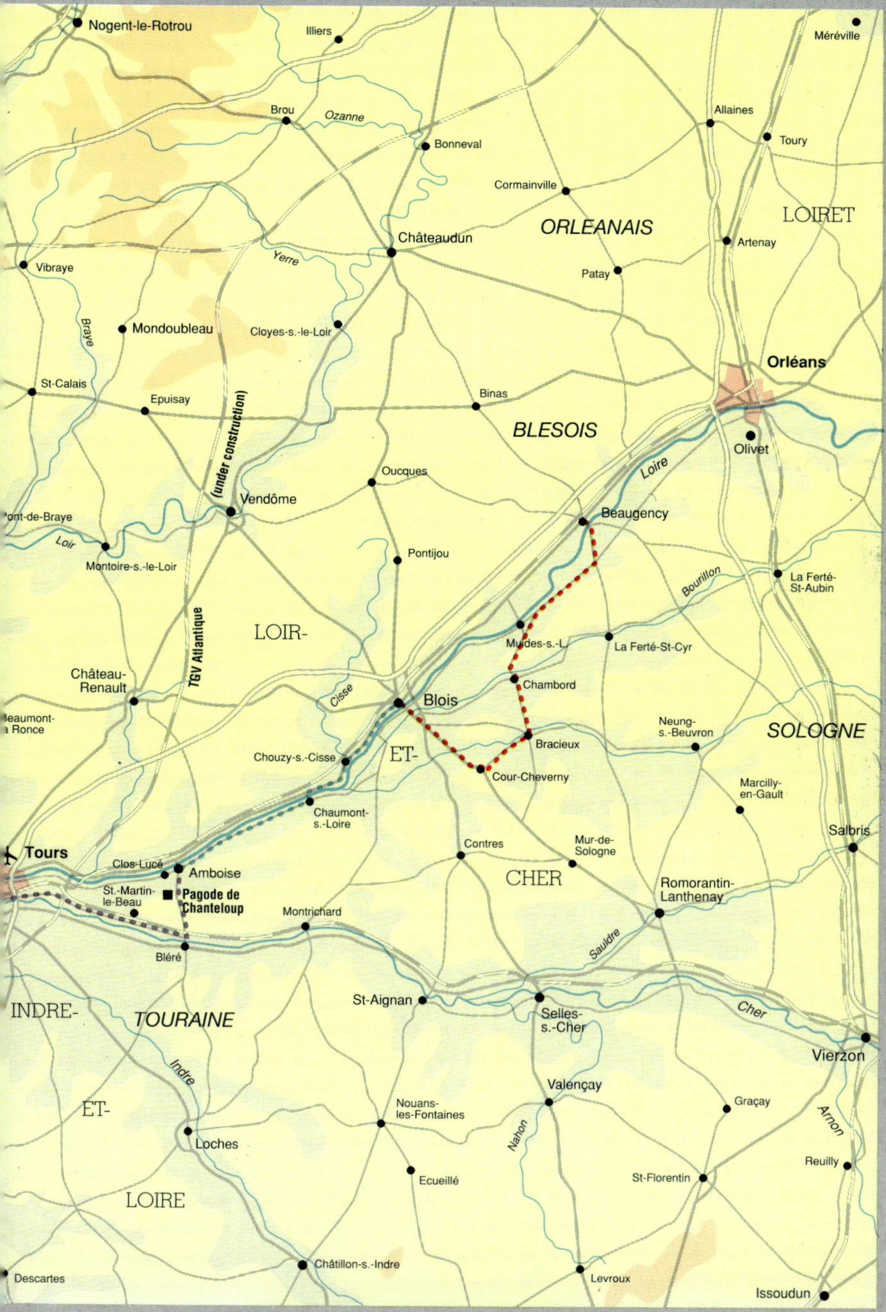
Nogent-le-Rotrou
Illiers
Méréville
Brou
Ozanne
Bonneval
Allaines
Toury
Cormainville
ORLEANAIS
LOIRET
Châteaudun
Artenay
Yerre
Patay
Vibraye
Braye
Mondoubleau
Cloyes-s.-le-Loir
Orléans
St-Calais
Epuisay
(under construction)
Binas
BLESOIS
Olivet
Loire
Oucques
Vendôme
Beaugency
Pont-de-Braye
Loir
Montoire-s.-le-Loir
Pontijou
Bourillon
La Ferté-St-Aubin
TGV Atlantique
LOIR-
Muides-s.-L.
La Ferté-St-Cyr
Château-Renault
Cisse
Blois
Chambord
Beaumont-la Ronce
Neung-s.-Beuvron
SOLOGNE
Chouzy-s.-Cisse
ET-
Bracieux
Cour-Cheverny
Marcilly-en-Gault
Chaumont-s.-Loire
Salbris
Tours
Contres
Mur-de-Sologne
Clos-Lucé
Amboise
CHER
Romorantin-Lanthenay
St.-Martin-le-Beau
Pagode de Chanteloup
Montrichard
Sauldre
Bléré
INDRE-
TOURAINE
St-Aignan
Selles-s.-Cher
Cher
Vierzon
Indre
Valençay
ET-
Nouans-les-Fontaines
Graçay
Arnon
Loches
Nahon
Ecueillé
Reuilly
St-Florentin
LOIRE
Châtillon-s.-Indre
Descartes
Levroux
Issoudun

INSIGHT *Pocket* GUIDES

LOIRE VALLEY

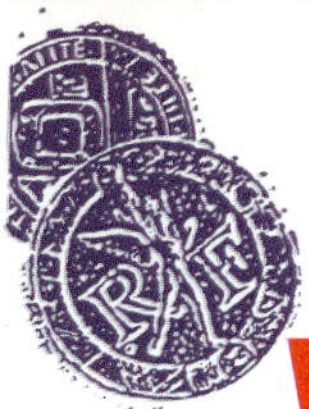

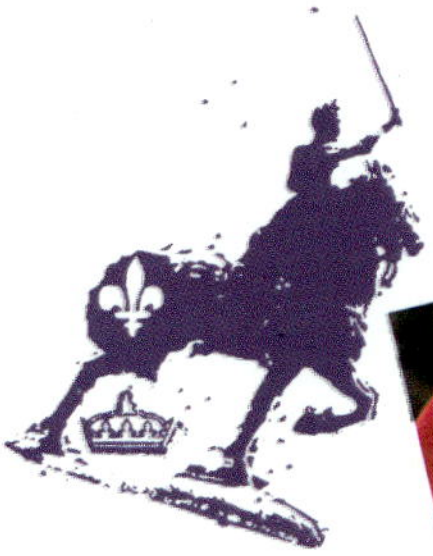

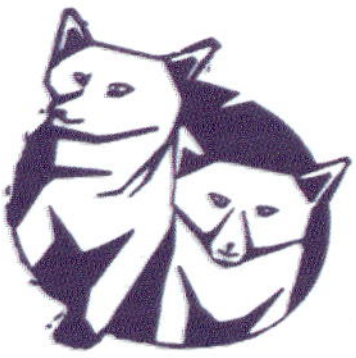

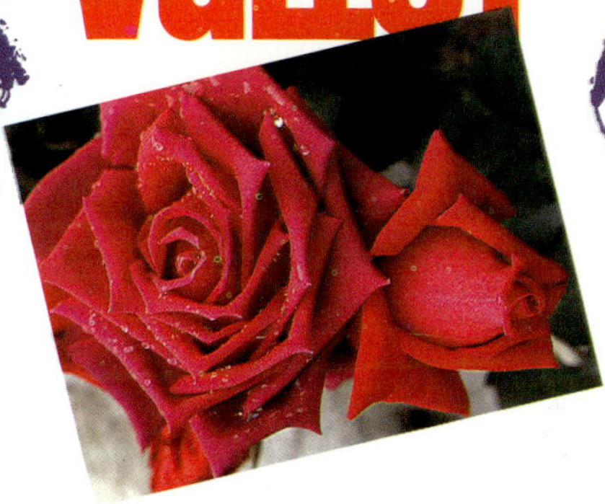

Written and Presented by **Lisa Gerard-Sharp**

Insight Pocket Guide:
LoireValley

Directed by
Hans Höfer

Editorial Director
Andrew Eames

Photography by
Lyle Lawson

Design Concept by
V. Barl

Design by
Klaus Geisler

© 1993 APA Publications (HK) Ltd

All Rights Reserved

Printed in Singapore by
Höfer Press (Pte) Ltd
Fax: 65-8616438

Distributed in the United States by
Houghton Mifflin Company
2 Park Street
Boston, Massachusetts 02108
ISBN: 0-395-65764-4

Distributed in Canada by
Thomas Allen & Son
390 Steelcase Road East
Markham, Ontario L3R 1G2
ISBN: 0-395-65764-4

Distributed in the UK & Ireland by
GeoCenter International UK Ltd
The Viables Center, Harrow Way
Basingstoke, Hampshire RG22 4BJ
ISBN: 9-62421-551-0

Worldwide distribution enquiries:
Höfer Communications Pte Ltd
38 Joo Koon Road
Singapore 2262
ISBN: 9-62421-551-0

NO part of this book may be reproduced, stored in a retrieval system or transmitted in any form or means electronic, mechanical, photocopying, recording or otherwise, without prior written permission of Apa Publications. Brief text quotations with use of photographs are exempted for book review purposes only.
As every effort is made to provide accurate information in this publication, we would appreciate it if readers would call our attention to any errors that may occur by communicating with Apa Villa, 81 The Cut, London SE1 8LW. Tel: 71-620-0008, Fax: 71-620-1074. Information has been obtained from sources believed to be reliable, but its accuracy and completeness, and the opinions based thereon, are not guaranteed.

Bienvenue!

Welcome! My childhood memories of the Loire Valley are coloured by unfortunate pen-friend exchanges: too much *lycée* and too little *liberté*. However when I worked in Brussels and Paris as a journalist and broadcaster the Loire Valley became the ideal place to escape.

From Paris, the Loire Valley is seen as a bastion of Vieille France, with minds as cultivated as Renaissance gardens. To the Parisians, the Loire has cachet. It is home to a serene, bourgeois, even indolent business class. Yet just below the surface is a race of hardy peasants with the secrets of good wine, a Rabelaisian philosophy and that much-vaunted French asset: roots.

In *Insight Pocket Guide: Loire Valley* I take you on a riverside journey through the garden of France. Our route follows the Loire downstream from Beaugency to Saumur, with five day-long itineraries designed to unravel the classic Loire, from countless royal châteaux to medieval towns and historic abbeys. In the course of this gentle meander west, there are also chances to get away from the river in a number of optional itineraries following lesser-known tributaries. Either way, you will encounter colourful winegrowers and eccentric châtelains.

For the enquiring traveller, there is a troglodyte trail, while the active traveller can canoe down the river Thouet or sample a balloon ride over royal Blois.

The inhabitants of the Loire Valley are not averse to presenting their charms on a plate. A classic menu would feature Bourgueil of Chinon red wine with *coq au vin* or Vouvray with a fishy *friture de la Loire*. Balzac and Rabelais, Loire residents, lived to tell the tale of overindulgence. So may you. *Bonne chance!* — Lisa Gerard-Sharp

Contents

Welcome **5**
History & Culture **10**
   The Cultural Landscape..........................**10**
   The English Connection **12**
   The Château Period **12**
   The Valley Today **14**
   Joan of Arc..**14**
   Celebrity Châtelains **15**
   Historical Highlights **17**

Day Itineraries..**18**
Beaugency to Blois
Day 1: Gateway to the Loire **20**
   Option 1: Joan of Arc's Orléans..............**25**
   Option 2: La Beauce...............................**28**
   Staying In and Dining Out........................**31**
Blois to Amboise
Day 2: La Route Royale **32**
   Option 3: Vieux Blois..............................**36**
   Option 4: A Taste of the Sologne...........**38**
   Staying In and Dining Out........................**42**
Amboise to Tours
Day 3: Treasures of Touraine **43**
   Staying In and Dining Out.......................**48**
Tours to Chinon
Day 4: Garden of France **49**
   Option 5: Balzac Country **53**
   Option 6: Chinon and Bourgueil **55**
   Staying In and Dining Out........................**57**
Chinon to Saumur
Day 5: Spirit of Anjou **58**
   Option 7: The Troglodyte Trail...............**62**
   Option 8: Montreuil-Bellay **64**
   Option 9: Downriver to Angers..............**66**
   Staying In and Dining Out........................**69**

Shopping **70**
Eating Out **72**
Wine **76**

Nightlife **79**
Calendar of Special Events **81**

Practical Information
Travel Essentials **84**
   When to Visit 84
Getting There **84**
   By Air, By Sea 84
   By Train, By Road 85
Getting Around **85**
   By Train, By Coach, By Shuttle, By Car ... 85
Accommodation **86**
   Hotels 86
Business Hours **87**
   Banks, Châteaux and Museums 87
Media & Communication **87**
   Daily Press, Telephone 87
Activities **87**
   Ballooning 87
   Boating, Boule de Fort, Cycling, Fishing,
   Golf, Helicopter Flights 88
   Riding, Rural Visits, Walking,
   Wildlife Watching 89
Children **89**
Useful Information **90**
   Consulates, French Tourist Offices
   Abroad, Loire Tourist Offices 90
Further Reading **91**
Index **92**

Maps
Loire Valley IFC–1
France 2
Blois 20
Orléans 25
Tours 43
Saumur 60
Downriver to Angers 66
Wine Regions 76

The Cultural Landscape

The Loire Valley is supremely regal. From the Middle Ages until the 17th century it was the seat of royalty. Government from the centre of the kingdom made good sense but this was not the sole motive for seating the administration in the Loire. A peace-loving population, proximity to Paris, and a soft and sensual landscape swayed the balance. Presumably, the cultivation of full-bodied wines and a rich cuisine provided the sub-text.

The Loire Valley boasted a deeply civilised population even from the earliest times. St Martin made Tours the cradle of French monasticism in the 4th century. Under Charlemagne's rule, Tours thrived, becoming the cultural hub of his great empire. At the same time, Alcuin, the abbot from Northumbria, made Tours a noted artistic centre, with a scriptorium for illuminated manuscripts. The Capets, the first French royal line, settled in Orléans and the city soon rivalled Tours.

However, in the 12th century, under the Plantagenets, the itinerant royal court moved between Chinon and Angers. The Plantagenets are better-known for their internecine rivalry than their intellectual prowess. Architecturally, however, their influence still illuminates Angevin vaulted churches all over Anjou. The Plantagenet style approached perfection in Fontevraud Abbey and Cunault but its legacy also embraces the Loire *levées*, graceful floodbanks built by Henry II.

Orléans was France's intellectual capital in the 13th century, confirmed by the presence of the royal court. The *Roman de la Rose*, the most influential text in medieval France, was written by Guillaume de Lorris and Jean de Meung, both local writers. This allegory of courtly love encapsulates two strands of French thought: one lyrical yet refined, the other vigorous and satirical. These divergent approaches are later encountered in the works of

& Culture

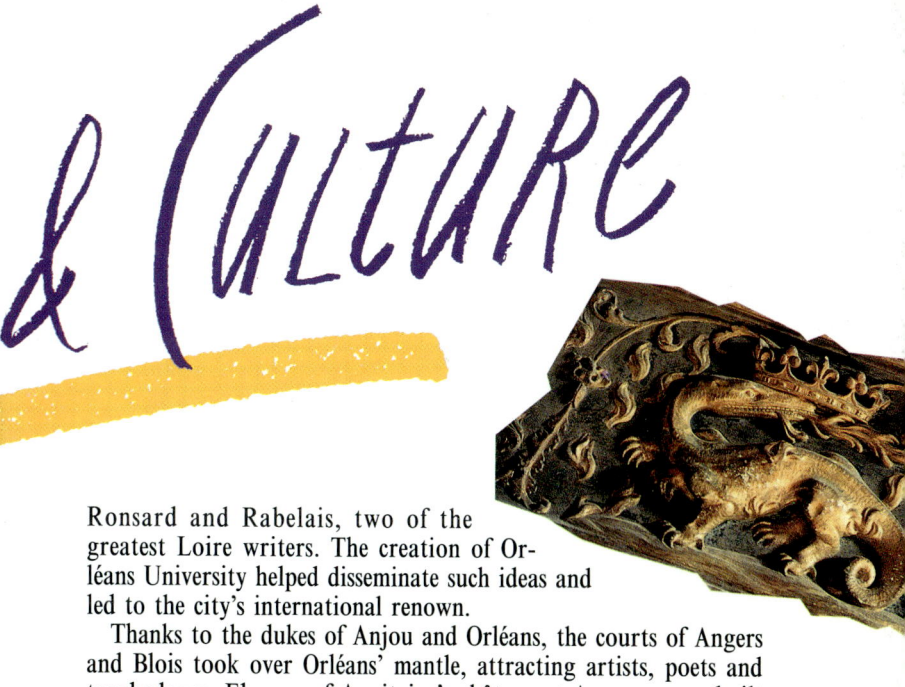

Ronsard and Rabelais, two of the greatest Loire writers. The creation of Orléans University helped disseminate such ideas and led to the city's international renown.

Thanks to the dukes of Anjou and Orléans, the courts of Angers and Blois took over Orléans' mantle, attracting artists, poets and troubadours. Eleanor of Aquitaine's château at Angers was rebuilt by the dukes of Anjou, notably Roi René (who was also King of Sicily), in the 15th century. François Villon, the greatest poet of the day, was invited to Blois by Charles d'Orléans. François I later extended a similar welcome to another outsider, Leonardo da Vinci, at Amboise.

The Loire Valley was riven by the Hundred Years War, fought on French soil. When not embroiled in battle, Charles VII divided his time between the fortresses of Chinon and Loches, where he fell under the spell of Agnès Sorel, the royal favourite. After Joan of Arc's death, Charles retired to Loches. His son, Louis XI, was

The Hundred Year's War from a 15th-century chronicle

The English Connection

The Plantagenets acquired their name from the *genêt*, the sprig of broom sported in their hats. Henry Plantagenet's marriage to Eleanor of Aquitaine united his lands (Anjou, Maine, Normandy and Touraine) with hers (Auvergne, Gascony, Poitou and Aquitaine). With Henry's accession to the English throne in 1154, French and English destinies were to be united for over 200 years.

As King of England, Henry II based his court in Angers but made Chinon the capital of his empire. His château, known as St George, was France's largest fortress. Henry II died in Chinon in 1189, as did his son, Richard the Lionheart. From Chinon, Richard's body was taken to Fontevraud Abbey, the traditional burial place of the Plantagenet kings.

To see Chinon as it was in the Plantagenets' time, go to the city's medieval market in August. The festivities cover the bridge which was built as a gesture of reconciliation between Henry II and his son, Richard. The Plantagenet legacy lies in Angevin castles and churches, notably Chinon's castle and St Maurice church. Other notable Angevin churches are in Asnières, Bourgueil, Cunault, Candes-St-Martin and Saumur. With some pride, locals regard the Plantagenets as French: Henry II and Richard the Lionheart lived longest in Anjou.

brought up there, but on succeeding to the throne he turned Loches into a prison and lived instead in Amboise and Plessis-les-Tours, a fortified manor on the outskirts of Tours.

The Château Period

Not until the reign of Charles VIII, Louis XI's son, do feudal castles give way to elegant Renaissance châteaux. By his marriage to Anne of Brittany in 1491 Charles VIII gained new lands and brought stability to France. Draughty Amboise was domesticated with the addition of comfortable royal wings and a great library; the Italianate gardens and ornamental terraces embodied Renaissance ideals in bricks and mortar. Charles' reign heralded a period of sustained châteaux-building, continued by Louis XII, his wise successor. Louis transformed Blois into a homely palace and it remained the administrative capital of France until the 17th century.

Louis' pious daughter Claude married François d'Angoulême, Renaissance scholar and future king of France. François I found

Chambord, the most majestic of the Loire châteaux

The Court of François I

Blois restrictive so built Chambord, the largest and most majestic of the Loire châteaux. Rabelais, born near Chinon, mocked Chambord as a great white elephant. The writer shook the whole 16th century with his breadth of vision but his rumbustious satire appealed to the emerging *haute-bourgeoisie* and the king.

François I's reign set the tone for an administration of enlightened self-interest. The new élite used their profits from the silk trade and banking to indulge in châteaux-building and patronage of the arts. The lovely châteaux of Azay-le-Rideau, Chenonceau and Villandry date from this period.

Azay and Chenonceau, the most romantic, were built by noblewomen whose husbands were away in battle. The accession of Henri II in 1547 marked the apogee of Renaissance excess, with Diane de Poitiers, Henri's mistress, running Chenonceau as a pleasure palace. Catherine de Médicis, Henri's wife, plotted Diane's downfall with her Italian astrologer in Chaumont. Her other political tool was the infamous flying squad, ladies of dishonour who would stop at nothing to spy for Catherine. While Regent of France, Catherine presided over a debauched court. Transvestite parties, nude balls and scurrilous poetry were distractions from grim affairs of state.

Fin de siècle decadence coincided with the end of the Valois dynasty and the decline of the Loire as a political centre. Ruggieri, Catherine's astrologer, had predicted this, as well as the tragic deaths of her three sons. In the 17th century France was torn apart by the Wars of Religion and the royal court left the Loire for Paris. From then on, the Val de Loire became a pleasant backwater, providing fables for La Fontaine, a racy salon for Madame de Sévigné and occasional hunting for Louis XIV at Chambord. The Loire did not escape the French Revolution of 1789 unscathed but thanks to the popularity of individual *châtelains*, many châteaux were spared, including Chenonceau and Cheverny.

Alfred de Vigny's family was not so fortunate. The poet's ultra-royalist parents lost their lands in the Revolution and were imprisoned in the Château de Loches. De Vigny celebrated his misty-eyed landscape in prose but never returned in person. But the 19th-century view of the Loire Valley is coloured by Balzac, Touraine's greatest novelist. Inspired by the romantic landscape, Balzac combines rhapsodies over ruined watermills with a meticulous portrait of provincial life. The hemp fields at Bréhemont disappeared with World War I but Balzac's view of village life lingered, as did the village *curé* and harvest festivities. Balzac's universe occasionally resurfaces in rural markets, old crafts and wine fairs.

On the eve of World War II, the Loire was still half rural, half historical relic. During the War, the valley formed the border between Occupied and Vichy France. The Château de Chenonceau's bridge over the Cher linked both camps. German and Allied bombing devastated Orléans, Tours and Saumur. However, in Saumur a handful of unarmed cavalry school cadets held off a Panzer division for two days. Reconstruction of the war-damaged areas continued into the 1960s, with whole quarters of Orléans re-invented from old photographs and memories.

The Valley Today

The Loire only finally recovered when France's decentralisation programme brought new prosperity to the region. Heavy industry was rejected in favour of plastics, pharmaceuticals and perfumery. While the Loire is no Silicon Valley, hi-tech and electronics industries do flourish in Gien, Tours and Orléans. Michelin tyre factories exist in Tours and Orléans. Major defence, armaments and aero-

Joan of Arc

Joan of Arc, the maid of Orléans, is France's best-loved saint, particularly in the Loire, her adopted homeland. It was by the grand fireplace in Chinon that the 17-year-old peasant girl first met the Dauphin Charles. Later, Joan convinced Charles to go to Rheims to be crowned. She swore to avenge the French defeat by the English at Agincourt and the burning of Notre Dame de Cléry. Victory in 1429 at Orléans was her greatest triumph.

By 1428 France was divided: the English controlled the west and held Paris while the Burgundians ruled the east. The Dauphin, derided as 'le petit roi de Bourges,' barely controlled the land south of the Loire. To complete their conquest of France, the English had to become masters of the Loire so, with the Burgundians, they besieged Orléans. However, in 1429 Joan of Arc entered the encircled city and rallied the French forces. During the battle, she was struck by an arrow and the English cry went up: 'The witch is dead'. But they were mistaken. Lord Salisbury, leading an army of 10,000 men, was killed and Joan led the French to victory. She then escorted the Dauphin to Rheims to be crowned.

However, the Maid of Orléans did not succeed in her avowed aim of 'kicking the English out of France'. After failing to regain Paris, she was captured at Compiègne and burned at the stake at Rouen in 1431. Her martyrdom is not forgotten in Orléans: her liberation of the city is re-enacted every May in a ceremony often attended by the French President.

nautics installations are tucked away in rural Sologne and Berry. The Loire is also home to *haute-couture* fashion: Christian Dior and Christian Lacroix are based in Orléans. The food industry processes meat, cheese, chocolates and, horror, ready-made meals.

The local wine trade ranks fifth in national importance but, as its wines improve, it is gaining prestige. Large-scale farming is restricted to the wheatfields north of Orléans. Elsewhere, the flight from the land has left idyllic villages vulnerable to Parisian purchasers of *résidences secondaires*. Fast TGV trains bring Paris within easy reach of Orléans commuters. Thanks to its industrial base and proximity to Paris, the Loire's official capital is now Orléans. But culture and quality of life make Tours the natural visitors' capital, with Angers a close second.

After the Revolution, the old provinces of Berry, Blésois, Orléanais and Touraine were divided into six confusingly-named *départements*. To complicate matters further, Anjou is technically excluded from the region blandly rechristened Région du Centre in 1972. This book uses the names of the old provinces since they carry more resonance and are still in common use: Région du Centre designates the *Val de Loire*, an area the size of Belgium.

The Loire has produced noted pastoral writers, of whom the best is Maurice Genevoix. In lyrical prose, he captures the wildlife and watery landscape of the Sologne as well as the moody river Loire. In summer, France's longest river is more sand than water. Writer Julien Gracq says that the micro-climates on the Loire make it 'a type of Orinoco or Senegal' in its profusion of exotic wildlife. The sculpted sandbanks are a breeding ground for tropical plants. These spring up from grain dropped by migratory birds or from passing barges which once plied their trade along the Loire.

After the project to dam the Loire was shelved in 1990, ecologists and nature-lovers breathed a sigh of relief. Kingfishers, herons and terns should be safe for another generation even if riverside dwellers are not. Jean Royer, Mayor of Tours, continues to fight for the dam, insisting that the Loire's unpredictable floods put the riverside population at risk. Feelings are so strong that the dam project may yet be revived. At the heart of it is a conflict between interventionists who undervalue nature and citizens who mythologise its untramelled power.

Celebrity Châtelains

Politics in the Loire tend to be conservationist and conservative. Given its royalist past and its role as epicentre of the French Renaissance, this is understandable. The landed aristocracy enjoys a status out of proportion to its size. In 1989 Louis Alphonse, Duke of Anjou and Bourbon, was proclaimed Louis XX, rightful heir to the throne. More typical, however, are the entrepreneurial *châtelains* who struggle to make their inherited stately homes profitable.

In the Château de Briottières, François de Valbray tempts paying guests with wine-tasting sessions and late-night Calvados. After inheriting the Renaissance Château des Réaux, Florence de Bouillé lived without electricity for two years. Florence proudly boasts that her husband installed 18 bathrooms with his own hands. Even today, while paying guests sleep in Renaissance suites, the couple are reduced to a sofa-bed in the converted dungeons.

At the other end of the scale, Jean St-Bris, aristocratic owner of Clos-Lucé, represents the new breed of *châtelain*. This marketing supremo transformed his manor house into a Leonardo da Vinci museum which attracts over 200,000 visitors a year. In the Château d'Ussé the Marquis de Blacas hit upon the idea of staging a *Sleeping Beauty* display in the turrets and charging the highest entry fee in the Loire.

But the high-profile *châtelains* are just one face of the Loire, and not the best-loved. Jean Chamboissier, Mayor of Bourgueil, talks animatedly of the ordinary folk who put a spoke in the wheel of history. His reserves his praise for the wife of Thibault-le-Tricheur who poisoned her wicked husband, or for the poacher who stole his master's game. In the valley of the kings, it is accessible people who are admired and those who are close to nature. In a land of anti-heroes, characters such as Rabelais and Gérard Depardieu reign.

As a child growing up near Chinon, Depardieu's friend actor Jean Carmet recalls 'playing Gargantua', reconstructing the Giant's war over Touraine, a landscape both fictional and real. Mick Jagger now plays at being a *châtelain* at Amboise while Depardieu himself acts the *vigneron* in Anjou. Both Depardieu and Carmet are *fils du pays*, local boys. Carmet says of Depardieu, 'Gérard became a wine-grower out of a passion for wine and companionship: sharing his traditional wine with friends is his idea of bliss.'

Good wine and food go hand in hand in the gourmet's Loire. After listening to local speeches on the glorious wine, landscape and *douceur de vivre*, you may detect a touch of smugness in this bourgeois paradise. If so, it is justifed. Angers and Blois regularly top French surveys on the quality of life. This dream ticket of traditional landscape and rich lifestyle is deeply coveted, and not just by the French.

Mick Jagger's château

Historical Highlights

BC
1000–600 Celtic tribes settle in Gaul.
59–51 Julius Caesar conquers Gaul.

AD
Circa 250 St Gatien introduces Christianity to France.
4th Century St Martin, Bishop of the Gauls, founds Marmoutier Abbey near Tours and dies in Candes in 397.
732 Charles Marcel defeats the Saracens near Tours.
814 Death of Charlemagne.
9th century Norman invasions reach Angers and Tours.
987 Hugues Capet founds Capetian dynasty, the first French royal family.
1104 First Council of Beaugency excommunicates Philippe I.
1152 Second Council of Beaugency annuls marriage of Louis VII. Henry Plantagenet marries Eleanor of Aquitaine.
1154 Henry Plantagenet becomes King of England as Henry II.
1189 Henry II dies at Chinon. The Court is centred on Chinon and Angers.
1204 King John, the last Plantagenet king, loses Anjou.
1305 First university of Orléans founded.
1337 Hundred Years' War: English victories at Crécy (1346) Calais (1347), Agincourt (1415).
1417 Henry V advances. Dauphin Charles withdraws to Bourges.
1422–1461 Charles VII. Court based at Loches.
1427–8 English invade the Loire and besiege Orléans.
1429 Orléans liberated by Joan of Arc. Dauphin is crowned as Charles VIII.
1431 Joan of Arc burnt at the stake at Rouen on 30 May.
1453 English lands in France reduced to Calais and Guines.
1491 Charles VIII marries Anne of Brittany at Langeais.
1496 The Renaissance influence spreads from court at Amboise.
1498–1515 Rule of Louis XII. Court based at Blois.
1515–47 Rule of François I. The Court is based at Blois and Chambord.
1519 Leonardo da Vinci dies at Clos Lucé, Amboise.
1560 Amboise Plot by Protestants. Death of François II.
1560–98 Wars of Religion. Beaugency and Vendôme sacked.
1598 Royal court leaves the Loire forever.
1685 Edict of Nantes revoked: Protestants flee from Saumur.
1643–1715 Rule of Louis XIV. Court now based in Versailles.
1789 French Revolution. Orléans University destroyed.
1815 Bourbon Restoration. Amboise and Chambord return to their pre-Revolutionary owners.
1832 First steamboat on the Loire.
1845 Tours–Orléans railway opens the Loire to new trade.
1870–1 Franco-Prussian War.
1939–45 Orléans, Saumur and Tours suffer bomb damage. The Loire marks the division between Occupied and Vichy France.
1969 New universities at Orléans and Tours. Nuclear power stations come on stream at Avoine (1969) and St Laurent (1974).
1989 Opening of the TGV Atlantique, linking the Loire to Paris.
1992 Loire Valley nuclear power stations to close.

Day It.

The Loire Valley is one of the most popular French regions: Chenonceau is the biggest attraction in France after Versailles. While the major sights are crowded in summer, just off the royal châteaux trail the valley is surprisingly tranquil. Clever scheduling ensures peace and quiet: in the case of the major châteaux, an early morning visit favours privacy. By contrast, the loveliest Loire towns, such as Blois and Saumur, are most appealing in the late afternoon and early evening. In many châteaux, guided tours are compulsory: unless you happen to speak good French, request a spoken or written translation (neither are automatically provided).

Saumur

Itineraries

Châteaux are usually good value, with entrance fees of 25–35 francs. State-owned properties tend to be cheaper than private ones. Villandry and Ussé are more expensive: the former includes magnificent gardens and a tour while the latter is merely greedy. Individual events within the châteaux may be charged separately: horse displays (at Chambord); boat trips (at Chenonceaux). Some towns have discount tickets for a selection of local sights.

The following itineraries presume a car but also allow for walking tours and even boat trips. Apart from motorway intersections in the major cities, roads are well-signposted, particularly to major attractions. Since some routes cover places that are off the beaten track, a good map is essential. The one recommended is the Institut Géographique National (IGN) Val De Loire (number 106).

This book's journey down the Loire is divided into 5 regions, each with its own full-day itinerary and related optional itineraries. Each region also has its own self-contained section on dining and accommodation, *Staying In & Dining Out*; principal restaurants and hotels mentioned in the itineraries themselves are detailed in full in *Staying In & Dining Out*.

The 5 full-day itineraries hug the river Loire from Beaugency to Saumur. These classic days out form the royal route through châteaux country, ending each day in an historic town. This main menu is supplemented by the Loire *à la carte*, 12 optional itineraries that explore the lesser-known paths across the plains, vineyards and troglodyte villages.

Beaugency → Blois

Day 1

Gateway to the Loire

This full-day excursion follows the Loire downriver from the medieval town of Beaugency to Blois, the most appealing of the larger Loire towns. En route, you will visit the contrasting Châteaux of Chambord and Cheverny. A gentle drive through the forest leads to the new base at Blois. A stroll through the old quarter ends in a leisurely dinner and a 'son et lumière' at the Château de Blois.

Ideally, you will have arrived in **Beaugency** late the previous afternoon and glanced at the old quarter prior to dining in a regional restaurant. Before collapsing into bed, at least walk down to the river, a stone's throw from the hotel. From the banks of Quai de

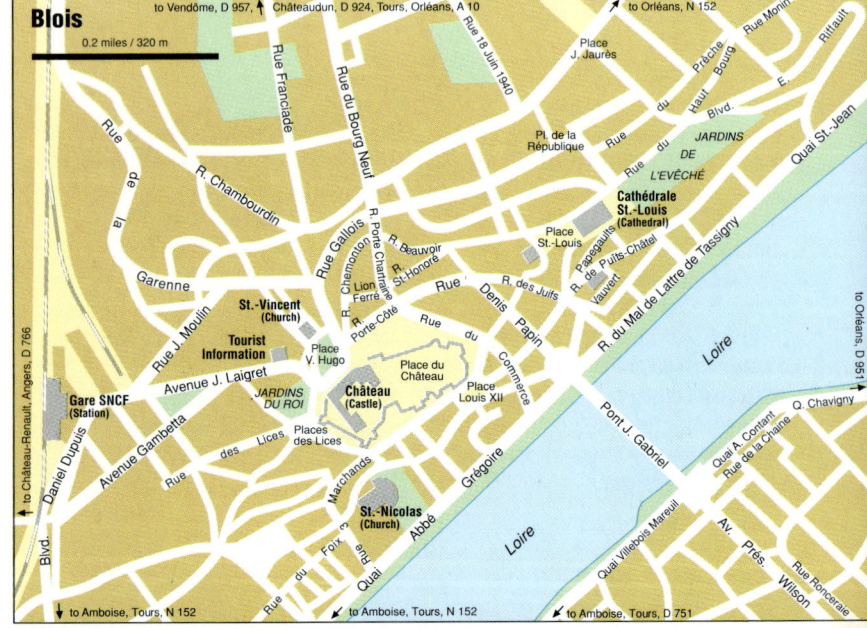

Beaugency, tranquil after centuries of turmoil

l'Abbaye there is a view of the **medieval bridge** which separates the wheatfields of la Beauce from the watery landscape of la Sologne. This is known as 'the Devil's Bridge' since legend has it that the Devil agreed to its construction in exchange for the soul of the first creature to cross it. The victim was a cat so citizens of Beaugency are often known as 'les chats,' free spirits. Beaugency has long been the gateway to the Loire, both a warm welcome and a portcullis protecting the royal châteaux.

During the Hundred Years' War, Beaugency fell into the hands of the English four times, only to be delivered by Joan of Arc in 1429. As a river fortress, it owed its prosperity to the Loire fleet until the last century. Make the most of the waterside views because, strange though it may seem, the Loire is rarely so accessible. It remains the last wild river in Europe and for much of your journey, it will be protected by huge stone *levées* or banks. Sit by the river's edge and you will see the Devil's tower looming above, with the austere abbey trapped like a fleeing monk in the moonlight.

Your day begins with a wander around the centre, beginning in **Place St Firmin**. By moonlight it, too, is dramatic, with its decapitated castle keep, belltower and statue of Joan of Arc on horseback. Daylight reveals a mellower stone square bedecked with flowers. At the far end is **Château Dunois**, a Renaissance manor house built on the site of the feudal castle. Walk into the courtyard to admire the elegant facade and, if you are staying more than a day in Beaugency, come back to visit the excellent regional museum inside.

Facing the Château is **Notre Dame**, the former abbey church. At intervals, you will hear the famous carillon chimes of 'Orléans! Beaugency! Notre Dame de Cléry, Vendôme, Vendôme!' Joan of Arc's clarion call to arms. The Romanesque church, graced by a Gothic nave, has been the stage for royal as well as spiritual dramas. It was here that the marriage between Eleanor of Aquitaine

Chambord, largest of the Loire châteaux

and Louis VII was annulled, leaving Eleanor free to marry Henry Plantagenet, the future King of England. Before leaving the church, look up at the pilasters carved with phoenixes, symbols of eternal life.

From here, walk along the bustling Rue du Pont to the stream running through Rue du Rü, the quaint mill district. Turn left into Rue des Trois Marchands to look at the medieval clocktower and, just beyond, the Gothic **Hôtel de Ville**. The facade is Renaissance, adorned with the town arms, royal salamanders and the scallop shell symbolising the pilgrimage path to Santiago. Before leaving town, have a farewell drink at the **Crêperie de la Tour** (26 Rue de la Cordonnerie), a cosy spot in which to savour the town's quiet charm.

Chambord's staircase

Drive across the Gothic bridge and follow the D951 to Muides-sur-Loire, a tobacco-growing area by the river. From here, take the D112 through the forest to **Chambord**, the grandest château in the Loire (daily 9.30am–5.45pm). Poet Alfred de Vigny likened Chambord to Baghdad and Kashmir, with its 'blue domes and elegant minarets'. The mystery of the East is present in the château's surreal skyline, cupolas and chimney-tops carved out of shimmering stone that becomes whiter as it ages. The geometrical construction is a masterpiece of stone and slate, reputedly designed by Leonardo da Vinci, an adviser to François I.

Chambord's setting, in the heart of the forest, is also its *raison d'être*.

François I, a great huntsman, chose the game-filled forests as the site for his new palace. 'Allons chez moi' was how he casually invited guests to his *pied à terre*, the hunting lodge that was transformed into the king's bid for immortality. Second only to Versailles in size, the château has impressive vital statistics: over 450 rooms and 70 main staircases, as well as a fireplace for every day of the year. Chambord also prefigures Versailles in its lavish interior decoration. The highlight is the double spiral staircase on which two people can walk up or down simultaneously and never meet.

Not until you leave the château do you appreciate the sheer size of the estate, the largest in Europe. The 14,000-acre grounds cover woods, lakes and a game reserve favoured by French presidents. There is a controversial plan to build a Renaissance theme park on the edge of the grounds. This glass pyramid would portray the sights, sounds and smells of Renaissance times. At worst a travesty and at best a pale imitation, it cannot hope to compete with the magical views from the rooftop terraces. Here courtiers danced, gossiped and watched the progress of the hunt.

After spending a couple of hours at Chambord, consider lunching at L'Hôtel du Grand St Michel, just opposite the château. Specialities include game pâté, grilled salmon and refreshing Touraine Sauvignon wine. For a lighter lunch, drive on to **Cour-Cheverny** (D112) and enjoy rustic cuisine at Le Grand Chancelier, Place de l'Eglise. Alternatively, there is a perfect picnic spot on a grassy lawn just behind the village church. Cheverny produces its own wine which can

Cheverny epitomises classical elegance

be sampled in the tourist office by the Romanesque church. If this individualistic *vin de pays* appeals, call in at a couple of vineyards after visiting the château of Cheverny (9.15am–6.45pm).

While Chambord is dauntingly majestic, **Cheverny** is sober, classical, yet approachable. If it feels like a family home it is because it is lived in by the Vicomte de Sigalas, a descendant of the original owners. In 1634, Henri and Marguerite Hurault finished this dazzling white building, a celebration of their happy marriage. The Hurault's union was matched by the loyalty of their master craftsmen: Jean Mosnier, amongst others, painted and gilded the interior for 12 years. Inside are a succession of panelled rooms, covered with Spanish leather, tapestries and 17th-century paintings.

Most of the Loire châteaux lost their original furnishings during the Revolution but, thanks to the Hurault's cosy relationship with the villagers, Cheverny was spared. As a result, the interior has great presence, particularly the **Grand Salon** and **Chambre du Roi**. These airy rooms are decorated in a flamboyant style, with floating

23

Cheverny interior

nudes or battle scenes on the ceiling and canopied beds below. As for the private quarters, these still have a family feel, from the Hurault's rich library and family portraits to photos of the present generation, pictured at a Cheverny hunt.

Hunting plays an important role in the château's history and over 2,000 trophies are on display, including antlers reputedly 6,000 years old. After visiting the trophy room, wander over to the **kennels** and admire the hounds basking in the sun. The Cheverny hunt has a pack of 70 hounds that are used solely for stag-hunting. The dogs are a cross-breed between Poitevin and English foxhounds but, until feeding time, look deceptively sleepy. If you want to see them spring into action, watch the mass feeding at 5pm.

The Cheverny *son et lumière* (10.30pm) makes great play of the hunting connection, with a shepherdess presenting a staghunt and peasants portraying scenes from rural life. On the way out, notice the orangery where the *Mona Lisa* and other Louvre paintings were hidden during the War. If you enjoy wine, don't miss the

Cheverny hounds at the 5pm feed

chance of a *dégustation*. Cheverny Chardonnay is a young, quality table wine with a floral scent and honey note. Domaine des Huards, a typical Loire wine estate, offers light and fruity reds, dry whites and rosé (available from Michel Gendrier, Les Huards, Cour-Cheverny, Contres. Tel: 54 79 97 90). François Casin competes with a fruity, ruby-coloured Gamay (available from Le Petit Chambord, Cheverny. Tel: 54 79 93 75). It is often better to phone beforehand to check that the tastings are operating.

Alternatively, drive straight to **Blois** (D765) in the evening and try a Cheverny wine at dinner. After checking into your hotel, stroll around the old quarter. If you have the energy, follow the walking tour in *Vieux Blois (Option 3)*. But if Blois' gentle hills are too much for tonight, retire to an open-air dinner on Place Vauvert, an intimate medieval square, and conserve your energy for the atmospheric *son et lumière* at the château. There are at least two performances every evening (in English or French) but check the times posted outside the château or call at the tourist office (3, Avenue J Laigret. Tel: 54 74 06 49).

Option 1: Joan of Arc's Orléans

A half-day trip from Beaugency or Blois. Follow the 152 to Orléans and park in Place du Martroi.

Orléans may be one of the most famous regional capitals but it is the least typical of the Loire. Since Joan of Arc liberated it from the dreaded English in 1429, the city has been devastated by invaders, particularly in World War 2. Despite reconstruction of the historic quarters, the city feels elegant but hollow. Its critics even call it a suburb of Paris. However, Orléans is not as soulless as it

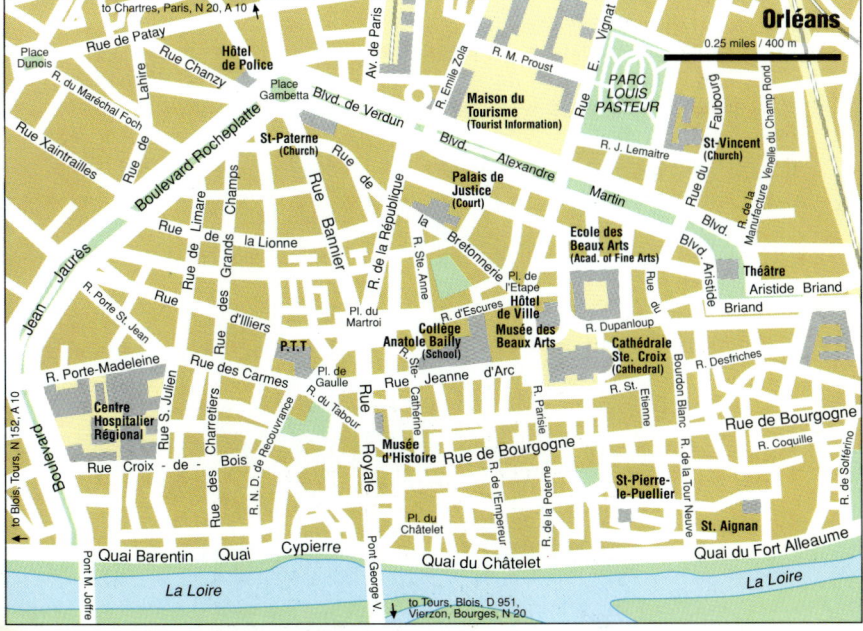

Orléans, an important regional centre and university town

looks, particularly if the Joan of Arc story has any resonance. Orléans has cultivated its old character, including an attachment to Joan of Arc and a militant republicanism which is at odds with its royal past.

The walk I suggest ignores the characterless suburbs and commercial centre and focuses on Vieil Orléans, the quarter bounded by Place du Martroi, the cathedral and the river. This patch also boasts churches, Renaissance mansions and an excellent Fine Arts Museum. Once on **Place du Martoi**, admire the equestrian statue of Joan of Arc, the highlight of this classical but distinctly windswept square. **La Chancellerie**, a *brasserie* on the square, is the place for a reviving glass of *vin d'Anjou*. If the spot appeals, come back later for a candlelit dinner on the terrace; fishy specialities include sole, monkfish and swordfish, not all caught locally.

From the square, walk along Rue d'Escures towards the Cathedral. Along the way, notice the 16th-century Eglise St Pierre and several Renaissance *hôtels particuliers*. The finest of these is **Hôtel**

Festival in Orléans

Groslot, on the right. Set in attractive gardens, this huge red-brick mansion was where François II died in 1560 after attending a meeting of the French Parliament with his bride, Mary Queen of Scots. But, in Orléans, saints are rated higher than queens: this former town hall honours Joan of Arc with a statue. The saint's costume is riddled with bullet-holes, not an English crime but the result of war damage.

Virtually opposite Hôtel Groslot is the **Musée des Beaux Arts** (10am–12am, 2pm–6pm; closed Tuesday). Here, traditional saints are honoured by Sienese and Flemish masters but there is scant reference to St Joan. Locals admire the collection for its coherent and chronological view of French art but outsiders are more impressed by the foreign masters and the broad-ranging modern collection. Exhibits include works by Renoir and Monet, Gauguin and Rouault, Picasso and Dufy.

Stained glass at Ste Croix

Outside, the **Cathédrale Sainte Croix** dominates the square and the skyline. The scale echoes Notre Dame de Paris but the spirit is strangely absent. While essentially Gothic, the cathedral has been remoulded in true Orléanais fashion. Its austere appeal lies in odd detail rather than in sheer vision. Highlights include 18th-century marquetry in the chancel, Byzantine enamels in the treasury and the late 19th-century stained glass windows, a homage to St Joan. Beginning on the left-hand side of the nave, you can follow her voices and visions to her burning by the English. Window number four shows Joan delivering Orléans while window eight shows her capture. Naturally, the French forces are models of elegance while the dastardly English are snub-nosed and plodding. Just behind the cathedral, the gardens of the former bishopric afford the best view of the delicate flying buttresses.

Orléans has a disconcerting habit of moving buildings to more prominent positions. Churches, pieces of city wall and medieval houses have been reassembled within the old quarter. A few streets away, on Place de Gaulle, the **Maison Jeanne d'Arc** has the virtue of remaining on its original site but has been rebuilt from pieces of neighbouring period buildings. Inside is a museum to the local heroine (10am–12am, 2pm–6pm; closed Monday).

From these attic windows, Joan once overlooked the English camp and Notre Dame des Miracles, the church that inspired her. From the museum, the energetic can visit two Romanesque churches between the cathedral and the river. **St Pierre Le Puellier**, the former university church, stages classical concerts. Outside, follow Rue des Africains east to **Cloître St Aignan**, a church with a striking Carolingian crypt. In Joan of Arc's time, the church was the largest in Orléans but the English burnt much of it before they retreated.

Before leaving town, wander through the pedestrianised area bordering **Rue de Bourgogne**, named after the second-most hated enemies of the Orléanais, the Burgundians. This charming quarter was largely spared during recent wars and retains a number of timber-framed houses. Rue de Bourgogne and the adjoining Rue Ste-Cathérine represent Orléans' stomach. For traditional cuisine, try **Chez Jean** (64 Rue Ste-Cathérine, Tel: 38 53 08 15). Orléans' fattening specialities include *terrines*, pâtés, chocolates and *Poire d'Olivet*, a pear-scented liqueur. For a night out, visit **Paxton's Head**, (264 Rue de Bourgogne Tel: 38 81 23 29), a popular bar and jazz club. Sadly, we have no evidence that Joan of Arc ate or slept here. Even if she had done, the locals would have changed the anglicised name and moved the building.

The plains of La Beauce are France's breadbasket

Option 2: La Beauce

This is a half-day trip off the beaten track from Beaugency (or Blois) to the cereal plains north of the Loire. A country drive leads to the isolated Château de Talcy, Romanesque churches and a windmill. From Beaugency, take the D917 for 8.5km (5¼ miles) to Josnes and join the D70 to Talcy (7km/4¼ miles). (Take a good map!)

La Beauce is the granary of France, a windswept landscape of corn, barley and sunflowers stretching north to Chartres. During the Wars of Religion, La Beauce was dotted with abbeys and its forests provided refuge. However, during the Revolution these abbeys, priories and châteaux gave way to stone farmhouses and vast plains.

The gentry moved away to grander châteaux on the Loire, leaving the feudal sharecroppers to become today's wheat barons. Today, placards in La Beauce protest against 'la France en friche', France laid fallow, but even in Ronsard's day the trees were being felled, much to the poet's chagrin. Yet La Beauce is no wasteland. Hamlets stand like islands of stone in the swaying wheatfields. Country lanes wind past workmanlike villages but in their midst are delicate chapels, walled manor houses, well-restored washhouses and lone windmills.

The **Château of Talcy** (9.30–11.15am, 2–6pm) is in the isolated village of the same name. It looms over the plains like a medieval fortress but appearances are deceptive; the building's feudal exterior hides a Renaissance heart. It was largely designed by Salviati, a Florentine merchant who favoured moody French Gothic over airy Italian *palazzi*. Wishing to be aloof from the royal court at Blois, Salviati transformed Talcy into a spiritual retreat and model farm. Even so, he was worldly enough to indulge in exquisite Renaissance furnishings, many of which still adorn the interior.

Surrounding the château are Renaissance gardens with traditional box borders and a rose garden. It was here that Ronsard wooed Salviati's daughter Cassandra, the inspiration for much of his poignant poetry. Salviati did not approve of an alliance between the impoverished poet and his 15-year-old daughter so Ronsard got no further than the rose garden. In the adjoining courtyard is a domed well and one of the loveliest dovecotes in France. The visit is accompanied by atmospheric music, cooing doves, chirping crickets and the squeaking of the château's ancient wine press.

After admiring the grounds, call in at the homely **Auberge du Château** (Tel: 58 81 03 14), just opposite the château, to sample such regional fare as cheeses and sausages. From here turn your back on worldly pleasures and take the D70 to the isolated chapels at **Villexanton** and **Villiers**. Both are Romanesque but while Villexanton offers a quaint timber-framed gallery, Villiers boasts 13th-century murals.

Just 1km (½ mile) west of Villiers is **Maves**, a 15th-century windmill

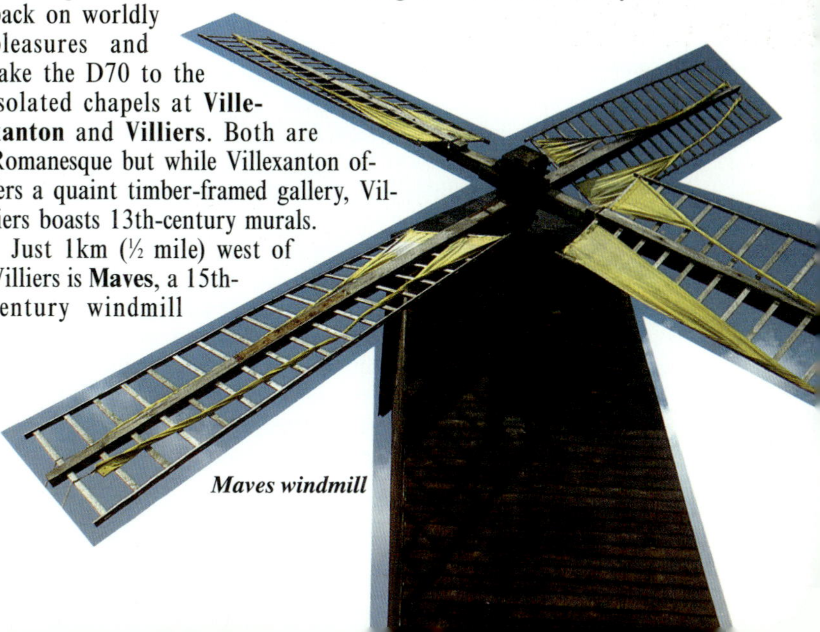

Maves windmill

on one of the bleakest spots on the plains. This working mill, one of 60 remaining, is a poor relation of the water mills in the lush Indre valley. Maves is conducive to sombre introspection but if you are tired of solitude, slip back to Beaugency along the north bank of the Loire.

Alternatively, a leisurely riverside route back satisfies a longing for conviviality and culture. From Maves, follow the D112 to another Romanesque church at Mulsans and take the D50 to Ménars, a classical château once owned by Madame de Pompadour. After glancing at the facade from the road, stop at **Cour-sur-Loire**, the next village north along the river. To appreciate one of the loveliest stretches of the Loire, sit by the river's edge and watch the fishermen, often in traditional black boats. Beside the river is a sloping Gothic church and, just behind, the ivy-covered village is picturesque with its lovingly-restored wash house and secluded château.

Follow the river north to **Suèvres**, a village in the heart of the asparagus-growing area. After glancing at the moated manor house and two Romanesque churches, continue north to Mer. Ignore this small market town and cross the river to **St Dyé-sur-Loire**, a celebrity village facing Suèvres. St Dyé owes its name to the patron saint of eyes, but owes its existence to Chambord. As Chambord's port, St Dyé shipped the stone that was used to build the Loire's largest château.

At the same time, St Dyé also acquired enough stone on its own account to construct a village church that was planned to be the size of Blois Cathedral. Sadly, the local stonemasons

Dovecote at Talcy

went on strike when they discovered that their Chambord counterparts were being paid more than they were; as a result the proportions of St Dyé's church today are relatively modest compared to what they could have been.

St Dyé's ramparts and sweeping river views have attracted artistic residents such as the Picasso and Cartier-Bresson families. Certainly, you will not be alone if you dine in **Le Manoir du Bel Air** (1 Route d'Orléans, Tel: 54 81 60 10). For an equally splendid view, drive 5km (3 miles) south to Chambord and dine in the **Hôtel St Michel**, overlooking the château (Tel: 54 20 31 31). From the sandbanks of St Dyé, follow the D951 back along the south bank of the river to cosy Beaugency.

30

Staying In and Dining Out

$$$$ Luxury
$$$ Expensive
$$ Moderate
$ Inexpensive

Beaugency

HOTEL DE L'ABBAYE DE BEAUGENCY
2 Quai de l'Abbaye, 45190 Beaugency.
Tel: 38 44 67 35.
Set in a converted abbey beside the river, in the town centre. Bedrooms (or suites) in former monks' cells. Atmospheric dining hall, bar and terrace. Classic French cuisine. *$$$.*

HOTEL DE LA SOLOGNE
Place St-Firmin, 45190 Beaugency.
Tel: 38 44 50 27.
Friendly, small hotel beside the tumbledown castle. Winter garden and charming terrace. Restaurants nearby. *$$.*

LE P'TIT BATEAU
54 Rue du Pont, 45190 Beaugency.
Tel: 38 44 56 38.
Bar/restaurant with regional cuisine and decor. *$$.*

Blois

CHATEAU DE COLLIERS
41500 Muides-sur-Loire.
Tel: 54 87 50 75.
16th-century château hotel on the left bank of the Loire, 15kms east of Blois. Pool, library, ponies. Dinner. *$$$$.*

LE RELAIS BLEU DU CHATEAU
22 Rue Porte Côte, Blois.
Tel: 54 78 20 24.
Welcoming central hotel at the foot of Château de Blois. Restaurant in quiet courtyard. *$$.*

MADAME JOUILLAT, AU VERT DOMAINE
Cormeray, 41700 Contres.
Tel: 54 44 31 17.
Chambres d'hôtes (B&B) in rustic farmhouse 10km (6¼ miles) south of Blois, near Château de Troussay. *$.*

LA BOCCA D'OR
15 Rue Haute, Blois.
Tel: 54 78 04 74.
Gourmet restaurant in heart of old Jewish quarter. *$$$$.*

L'ORANGERIE DU CHATEAU
1 Avenue J Laigret, Blois.
Tel: 54 78 05 36.
Formal restaurant in an orangery. Terrace overlooking the château. Fish and game. *$$$.*

LA MESA
11 Rue Vauvert, Blois.
Tel: 54 78 70 70.
On an intimate square in the centre of town. Eat indoors or under the trees. Slowish service. *$$.*

Chambord/Cheverny

HOTEL DU GRAND ST MICHEL
41250 Chambord.
Tel: 54 20 31 31.
Gorgeous setting opposite Château de Chambord. Excellent traditional cuisine (*$$$*), comfortable rooms. *$$.*

HOTEL DES TROIS MARCHANDS
Place de l'Eglise,
41700 Cour-Cheverny.
Tel: 54 79 96 44.
Village inn, regional restaurant. *$$.*

MARTINE THIMONNIER,
LA RABOUILLERE
Chemin de Marçon, 41700 Contres.
Tel: 54 79 05 14.
Chambres d'hôtes (B&B) in a typical farmhouse 10km (6¼ miles) south of Cheverny. (Just off D102). *$$.*

BLOIS → AMBOISE

DAY 2

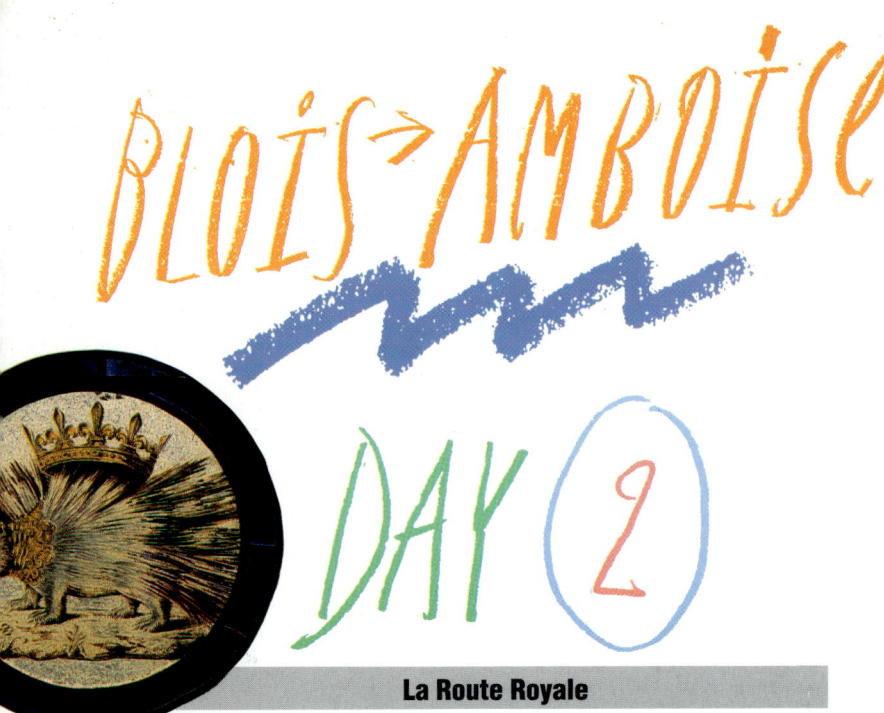

La Route Royale

This full-day excursion visits the Château de Blois and follows the Loire downstream to Chaumont. After lunch, we visit Leonardo da Vinci's manor at Amboise and walk around the town.

The Château de Blois, unlike Chambord, is both a haphazard configuration of styles and a resumé of French architecture. Seen from different angles, it is hard to fathom. From outside, it resembles an austere feudal castle. Viewed from the lush gardens below, it is an Italian palace: loggias jut out like boxes at the opera, treating the town as a court spectacle.

The château (9am–6pm) dates from the 13th century but only the Great Hall remains from then, sandwiched between the grander Louis XII and François I wings. The Louis XII wing is an uneasy blend of Gothic design tinged with Renaissance inspiration. It is adorned with the king's porcupine symbol and motto, 'From near and afar, I can defend myself'. As an absolute monarch, the king felt little need for protection, a view reflected in the openness of windows and balconies.

François demolished part of the Gothic castle but re-used the stone for this 'Versailles of the Renaissance'. His airy *palazzo* stretches between the feudal and classical wings. Look long at the spiral staircase, enveloped in an octagonal tower. Flaubert referred to it as 'cut out like the high collars of the *grandes dames* who walked the stairs 300 years ago.' Decorations include François' salamander, promising to 'encourage good and snuff out evil'. His pious wife loved Blois but François regularly abandoned both her and the château for the earthy pleasures of Chambord.

Château de Blois

During the Wars of Religion, Blois witnessed a dramatic turning point: the murder of the Duc de Guise by his rival Henri III in 1588. With Henri IV's reign, the court moved to Paris and Blois lost its political importance. Its last architectural flowering was in the 17th century when Louis XIII's brother, the exiled Gaston d'Orléans, built a new wing, an exercise in classical sobriety. The creation of Versailles meant the final eclipse of Blois.

The château is sparsely furnished but true to its origins, as are the paintings portraying its troubled history. One intriguing room is Catherine de Médicis' study, dotted with 237 secret cupboards, concealing jewels, state papers or potions. Still, nothing had any effect as the queen lay dying. According to the court chronicler, 'No more notice was taken of her than of a dead goat.' Instead of leaving Blois on this sombre note, have a farewell drink at the cheery bar next to the château.

Follow the RN152 on the north bank of the Loire and, just south of Onzain, cross the river to **Chaumont**. Before climbing the steep path to the château, enjoy a glass of Touraine from the terrace of **L'Hostellerie du Château**. This quiet spot is also an appealing choice for lunch, as is **Le Moutier du St-Martin**, a restaurant in a converted priory (Pont de Chaumont, Tel: 54 20 98 13).

The cliff-top **Château de Chaumont** (9.15am–5.35pm) is the highest of all Loire châteaux. Its cluster of towers is as bulky as a pregnant cat. On top of the windy cliff, there is a sense of space and wildness, with swishing trees and sweeping views. The hilly estate and forest trails are

Chaumont

wild but exciting. From the old stables, a bridge leads through a gnarled tree trunk into a wood of sweet-smelling cedar.

A castle has existed here since the 10th century, protected by moats, valleys and the river. Chaumont was 'lent' to Charles VII in 1431 and thereafter became crown property. Louis XI largely rebuilt it, softening the grim facades, and the 18th-century terraces were added in response to the French fashion for river views. Nonetheless, a feudal character remains in the sturdy towers and drawbridge.

Despite its beauty, Chaumont has rarely brought happiness. Catherine de Médicis, Henri II's widow, used it as a political pawn to humiliate her rival, Diane de Poitiers, the late king's mistress. By forcing Diane to accept Chaumont in return for her beloved Chenonceau, Catherine triumphed. But Catherine experienced despair at Chaumont: in her turreted observatory, she and her Florentine astrologer plotted the downfall of enemies. Here, Catherine read the grim destiny of her three sons, all to die violent deaths.

After you've lunched (see recommendations above), consider taking the 3pm river cruise from Chaumont (July to August only). Otherwise, follow the D751 along the south bank to Amboise and **Clos Lucé** (9am–7pm). After Chaumont, this compact brick and stone manor house is refreshingly domesticated. It was in this Renaissance home that François I played as a child and later, as king, installed Leonardo da Vinci. The wayward genius spent his last years here as 'Premier peintre, architecte et méchanicien du Roi'. In fact he acted as chief architect, civil engineer, court jester and king's confidant.

Clos Lucé is owned by the entrepreneurial St-Bris family, who realised that a Leonardo museum would draw the crowds. On display are models of his greatest inventions, from the helicopter to the plane, the machine gun to the tank. The spirit of commercial-

Clos Lucé, where Leonardo da Vinci worked and died

Silhouettes at Amboise

ism is rife, with gift shops and cafés in the rose gardens. Leonardo might have been prefiguring all this activity when he wryly commented: 'Doctors live upon the sick and friars upon saints long since dead'. Even so, the gardens stretch romantically down to the river and the sunny upstairs rooms are a loving evocation of Leonardo's time.

François I had a secret passage linking Clos Lucé to his **Château d'Amboise** (9am–6.30pm) but latter-day visitors need to drive or walk along Rue Victor Hugo. Before collapsing in a bar, call in at the château to book tickets for the *Spectacle Renaissance*, a sumptuous pageant (two shows a day, both in the evening) acted by local people which evokes a time when Amboise was the artistic centre of France. As home to five kings, Amboise is a most royal Loire residence. It was here that Charles VIII died in 1498, supposedly either from a poisoned orange or from hitting his head on a low doorway. Amboise today has lost several wings and its once glorious gardens. Even so, the ingenious riders' ramps, the delicate stone chapel and the river views are still visible. If you miss the evening show, consider visiting briefly in the morning.

Amboise itself is a chic town with gourmet restaurants patronised by celebrities like Mick Jagger, who owns a local château. The alleys below the château are bursting with choice. Simple *crêpes* and *andouillettes* are on offer at **Anne de Bretagne** (Rampe du Château). But to escape the crowds or prepare for a gourmet dinner in **Le Manoir St Thomas** (1 Mail St Thomas. Tel: 4757 22 52), walk across Quai de Gaulle and sit on a riverside bench. As the kayaks battle with the sandbanks, you may wonder whether Leonardo had pondered the problem and anticipated the solution: a dam.

Leonardo's tomb

Option 3: Vieux Blois

This short walking tour of medieval Blois is best in the afternoon or evening. The city turns its back on the river: few fine houses lie on the Loire. Instead, the town's old identity lies curled around the château.

An aerial view of Blois reveals a town hemmed in by forests. Before the feudal counts of Blois conquered the land, this was an inhospitable forest infested with wolves, the city emblem. These days the city still feeds off its forests, particularly in the hunting season, but Blois' unfriendliness has long since gone. Jack Lang, Blois' popular Mayor and Mitterand's Minister of Culture, has made the city a welcoming centre. The enlightened city council has marked intriguing walking tours along the 'Route Royale' and labelled key sites in English.

From the 14th century until the Revolution, the town followed the fortunes of the royal house. Thanks to this continuity, Blois has retained its old heart. It is only a quarter of the size of Tours yet the city has richer architecture, from the Jewish ghetto to grand *hôtels particuliers,* hidden courtyards and airy loggias. This is a place of exteriors, not interiors: museums and churches are secondary to the pleasures of traipsing up hilly streets and scouring alleys for fountains, royal emblems and cosy bars.

Beginning in **Place Louis XII**, at the foot of the château, admire the medieval fountain before strolling through the pedestrianised area around Rue du Commerce. From here, follow Rue Porte Côté to **Place Victor Hugo** and sit in the shaded garden to appreciate the elegance of the château above. Look through the fountains and willows to François I's Italianate loggia and, behind you, glance at St Vincent, a severe 16th-century church remodelled by the Jesuits.

Summon up the energy to explore the network of steep streets off Rue Porte Côté. Walk up **Rue Chemonton** and glance at the cluster of mansions once lived in by Louis XII's courtiers. Walk down

The old quarter

Rue Porte-Chartraine for similar sights and turn into **Rue St-Honoré** to see Hôtel d'Alluye, Blois' most authentic brick-and-stone Renaissance mansion. (Ring the bell of number 8 to be let into the courtyard.) From here, walk along Rue Beauvoir for views of sculpted doorways and the remains of the medieval castle.

Place St-Louis, the elegant cathedral square, soon comes into view. Once the town marketplace, this harmonious square boasts 18th-century facades, balconies and Blois' finest half-timbered house. This **Maison des Acrobates** features acrobats and jugglers, characters from medieval farces, sculpted on the facade.

The **Gothic cathedral**, backing on to the square, survived a hurricane in 1678. The eerie Romanesque crypt is the most atmospheric spot: while you absorb the vaulted ceiling and sculpted columns, a disembodied voice echoes through the gloom, reciting the history of the crypt.

Set high above the town, the **cathedral** and **Hôtel de Ville** (town hall) represent the moral and civic heart of Blois. During the Occupation, both buildings were landmarks for aviators who risked their lives making secret landings. Now the Hôtel de Ville is home to Jack Lang and its terraced gardens see little more dramatic than picnics and impromptu games of *boule*. Facing the Hôtel de Ville is a sundial inscribed with the motto: 'Time moves on, our works stand still; while we have the time, let us use it to the good'. The liberal people of Blois see this as a pretext for masterly inactivity on the sunny terraces overlooking the Loire. Follow **Rue Pierre de Blois**, a brick-paved alley leading downhill to the 14th-century Jewish ghetto. Notice the covered Gothic passage linking two medieval houses: the moulded beams are sculpted with a fire-eating monster. **Rue des Juifs** also boasts delicate mansions, including the galleried Hôtel de Condé, with its Renaissance archway and deep inner courtyard. Judging by the names and advertising plaques in the doorways, Jewish psychoanalysts strike a chord with today's angst-ridden citizens. But there is little sign of angst in the chic galleries and bars.

Where Rue des Juifs meets **Rue des Papegaults**, a photogenic half-timbered house straddles both medieval streets. The most striking courtyard in Rue des Papegaults belongs to Hôtel Belot, a 16th-century house adorned with an external spiral staircase, barrel-vaulted loggias and *fleur de lys* designs. This twisting street leads to **Rue du Puits-Châtel** and the galleried Hôtel Sardini, decorated with sculpted royal emblems, including Louis XII's porcupine. Close by is a mansion with an octagonal tower, exposed Gothic staircase and a balcony straight out of *Romeo and Juliet*. When this atmospheric quarter is floodlit, householders find friendly prowlers in their Renaissance courtyards.

An alley to the left is a short cut to **Place Vauvert**, the most intimate square in Blois. On summer evenings, the square is carpeted with restaurants but nothing detracts from Hôtel Sardini's floodlit Renaissance facade, dominating the square. From Rue Vauvert, a small doorway leads to a sweet-smelling herb garden which once belonged to the Sardini, prominent Italian bankers. To complete the walk, consider a classical concert in the **Halle Aux Grains**, the medieval covered market (Place de la République, Tel: 54 74 20 82). To be close to the château, dine on the terrace of Le Duc de Guise (15 Place Louis XII), a lively Franco-Italian restaurant.

Option 4: A Taste of the Sologne

This full-day excursion leads southwards from Blois, a gentle drive through the Sologne. En route, you will visit a manor house, a rural museum and a romantic Solognot château. There are recommendations for an overnight stop near the lakes.

La Sologne stretches from Orléans all the way south to the river Cher. These insalubrious marshes were first drained by medieval monks who created ponds and planted woods and vines. The closeness of the royal court at Blois spurred courtiers to build gracious mansions and hunting lodges. François I's mother and wife were born in the Sologne so the king patronised its châteaux. Later, epidemics and wars ravaged the region and it was deserted for centuries. Leonardo da Vinci devised a clever drainage scheme which was

Life is taken at a gentle pace in the Sologne

never implemented so it was left to Napoleon III, of Solognot stock, to re-dig canals and replant the desolate landscape. Recently, market gardening, hunting and green tourism have revived the slumbering Sologne.

Yet, for an artificial region, the Sologne feels deeply natural. The secretive landscape is one of dark woods and misty lakes, slender-spired churches and isolated inns. Low-roofed farms guard market gardens of irises, strawberry fields and asparagus beds. Timid wildlife and clog-wearing country-folk are equally mistrustful of outsiders. Stalk the locals carefully if you want to tease a conversation from a Solognot.

Follow the D956 to Cormeray and turn left to **Troussay** (10–12.30am, 2.30–6.30pm). This Renaissance dolls' house calls itself a 'gentleman's residence' and is still inhabited by a genteel couple. In the last century Louis de Saussaye, the Loire historian, restored Troussay by raiding local châteaux for their finest pieces. The stained glass windows and dining room fireplace of Troussay come from Blois while the carved oak chapel door comes from Bury. The effect is charming, from the cluttered kitchen to the warm, oval drawing room.

The small estate was once a model of self-sufficiency, with its own beehives, wine-press and weaving room. In the outbuildings is a collection of ploughs, harvesters' tools and beehives (a taste of a better rural museum to come). Troussay is dotted with worthy mottoes, including: 'Time flies so live the day to the full'. Wine-lovers should take this advice and visit the award-winning **Domaine Philippe Tessier** (Rue Colin, Tel: 54 44 23 82), 500m (547yds) from Troussay. The estate produces blackcurrant-scented whites and spicy, strawberry-scented reds.

From Troussay, take the D765 to **Mur-de-Sologne**, a village well-known for its game farms and wooded walks. (All the sights

Château du Moulin

below are within a 7km/4¼ mile radius of Mur.) Follow the D152 to **Veilleins**, a hamlet with typical timbered houses and L'Atélier du Sabotier, one of the last clog-makers in the region. From Veilleins, take the Lassay road to Etang de Bézard, Sologne's loveliest lake. En route, appreciate the forested **Tréfontaines estate**, with its château converted into a cheese farm (Tel: 54 83 86 27). If you feel like a picnic lunch, consider buying some goat's cheese. Further along the Lassay road, notice Manoir de la Motte, a 17th-century manor which was the French Resistance centre in the Loire.

At the **Etang de Bézard** the silence is ruffled only by the flight of wild ducks or the swirl of wading herons. By the 15th century there were 4,000 lakes in the Sologne and the monks kept the Paris markets supplied with fish. Today, carp, trout, perch, black bass, shrimps and eels are still fished in the local waters but many ponds have been turned into fish farms.

All local inns are rustic and inexpensive. **La Croix Blanche** in Mur-de-Sologne (Tel: 54 83 81 11) prides itself on its game menu. An alternative, in all senses, is **Château de Fondjouan** (Tel: 54 95 50 00), a novel organic restaurant. (From Mur, follow the D20 towards Gy.) Fondjouan residents also run courses on positive thinking. If this is too radical, try **Auberge du Prieuré** (Tel: 54 83 80 97) in Lassay-sur-Croisne, which specialises in *cuisine à l'ancienne*, hearty, old-style Solognot dishes.

After lunch, look at St Denis, Lassay's Gothic church, including its medieval mural of the Château du Moulin and the tomb of the château's first owner. From here, follow signs to **Château du Moulin** itself (9–11.30am, 2–6pm). The moated château was built by Philippe du Moulin, the knight who saved Charles VIII's life at the Battle of Fornova (1495).

The jocular guide belies the romance of the château, with its chivalric history, mysterious location and delicate red-brick turrets. Madame de Marchéville, the relaxed owner, is proud of her restoration work, but with 12 grandchildren of her own she is resigned to finding sticky finger-marks on her tapestries. Her bedroom boasts a canopied bed, scenes depicting rutting stags and a portrait of Isabelle d'Espagne which glows in the dark. The vaulted guardroom, the oldest part of the château, contains a spit which was pulled by dogs until they dropped from exhaustion; each meal cost the lives of three dogs.

From Lassay, follow the D20 north, turn off shortly towards Gy-en-Sologne and follow signs to the rural museum **Locature de la Straize** (10–11.30am, 3–6pm). Jean Picard, the clog-wearing owner, comes from a long line of peasants and is passionate about his museum. In local parlance *locature* means estate cottage and, given the difficulty of building on marshy soil, is always a humble, single-storey dwelling. This stone and timbered cottage is embedded with fossils, proof that this area was once underwater. A Solognot family all lived in one room, with the rest of the house used as a barn, hayloft and dairy.

In the modest living room it is a surprise to see canopied beds, even for babies. These were designed for health, warmth and privacy. Since this is the Sologne, secrecy is also endemic. To avoid paying the salt tax, salt was hidden in a hollow chair. Look out, too, for a woman's nightshirt with a hole in it. Solognot prudery meant that it was not done for a husband to see his wife's naked body. Mr Picard jokes that the hole was an effective form of birth control. A neighbouring wattle-and-daub cottage contains a small costume museum. To grasp the harshness of the Sologne, look at the period photographs showing the careworn faces of young girls.

Romorantin-Lanthenay

From here, take the D765 12km (7½ miles) to **Romorantin-Lanthenay** and end the day with a stroll around the old town. Park by the tourist office (Tel: 54 76 43 89) on Place de la Paix. If staying overnight, book a tour of a game, fish, goat or angora farm for tomorrow followed by an evening of Solognot songs and folklore.

Even if returning to Blois along the D765, it would be foolish to miss dinner in Romorantin, the gastronomic capital of Sologne. **Le Grand Hôtel du Lion d'Or** (62 Rue G Clemenceau, Tel: 54 76 00 28) is Sologne's star gastronomic restaurant. **Le Colombier** (18 Place du Vieux-Marché, Tel: 54 76 12 76) is a cosy inn noted for its rabbit, pheasant or pike in a mushroom sauce. Before dinner, walk along **Rue de la Résistance** with lovely mansions and the **Hôtel de Ville**, home to an excellent museum of local arts and traditions (10–11.30am, 2–5.30pm). Cross the bridge to the island and admire the view of mills, the Romanesque Eglise Notre Dame and the Rue de Venise.

Château de Chémery (Tel: 54 71 82 77) is a tumbledown castle run by enthusiastic Parisians which offers dinner and an overnight stay at good prices.

Romorantin architecture

Staying In and Dining Out

$$$$ Luxury
$$$ Expensive
$$ Moderate
$ Inexpensive

Amboise

CHATEAU DE PRAY
37400 Amboise.
Tel: 47 57 23 67.
13th-century château hotel in parkland above the Loire, 3km (1¾ miles) north-east of the town (off D751). *$$$*. Not too pretentious. Half-board obligatory in season. Dining *$$$$*.

HOTEL LE CHOISEUL
36 Quai Charles-Guinot,
37400 Amboise.
Tel: 47 30 45 45.
Classical riverside mansion set in Italianate gardens below Château d'Amboise. Pool. Panoramic gourmet restaurant. *$$$$*.

AUBERGE DU MAIL
32 Quai Général de Gaulle,
37400 Amboise.
Tel: 47 57 60 39.
Friendly, simple town hotel (*$*) with bistrot (*$$*) by D751.

MANOIR SAINT THOMAS
1 Mail St-Thomas, 37400 Amboise.
Tel: 47 57 22 52.
Elegant restaurant in Renaissance manor. Imaginative gourmet cuisine. Waiters in period dress. *$$$$*.

RESTAURANT L'AMBOISERIE
7 Rue Victor Hugo, 37400 Amboise.
Tel: 47 30 50 40.
Decor is an attractive mixture of old and new. Specialities of quiche, tournedos, stewed pike, Ste Maure cheese and local wines. *$$*.

Chaumont

DOMAINE DES HAUTS DE LOIRE
Route de Herbault,
41150 Onzain-en-Touraine.
Tel: 54 20 72 57.
18th-century waterside manor house in Onzain, 2km (1¼ miles) north of Chaumont. Rural hotel and classical French restaurant. *$$$$*.

HOSTELLERIE DU CHATEAU
41150 Chaumont-sur-Loire.
Tel: 54 20 98 04.
Comfortable hotel at the foot of the château. *$$$*. Terraced restaurant with regional and classical cuisine.

MADAME LANGLAIS (B&B)
46 Rue de Meuves, 41150 Onzain.
Tel: 54 20 78 82.
Chambres d'hôtes (B&B) in traditional house on river Cisse, 2km (1¼ miles) west of Onzain, on D58. *$*.

Amboise → Tours

DAY 3

Treasures of Touraine

This full-day excursion leaves the river Loire for the Cher. After visiting the Château de Chenonceau, we spend the afternoon exploring Tours, the capital of Touraine.

From Amboise, take the D31 through the forest of Amboise, stopping briefly at the **Pagode de Chanteloup**, a graceful piece of *chinoiserie*. This 18th-century pagoda was built by Louis XV's disgraced minister as a tribute to the friends who supported him in exile. From here, it is a short drive to **Chenonceau** (9am–7pm), the most popular château in the Loire. To see Chenonceau through a *châtelaine's* eyes, visit at opening time. At the end of a long line of

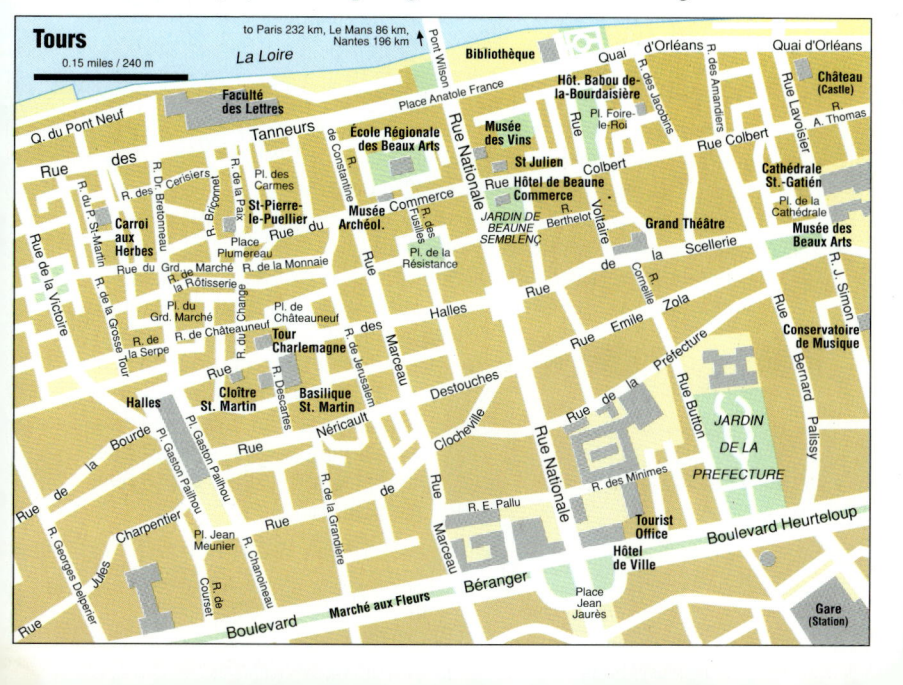

Chenonceau, most perfect of all the châteaux

plantain trees, the frothy white château comes into sight, a vista guarded by two sphinxes.

Chenonceau is the icing on the cake, the quintessential château. It comes as no surprise that its present owner is a *chocolatier*. Yet Chenonceau had little historical impact: compared with Blois, it was never a political pawn; unlike Orléans, it staged none of the set pieces of French history. Instead, Chenonceau was a pleasure palace and private theatre, fought over by a series of women owners but always loved for itself.

In 1513 Catherine Briçonnet supervised the initial building. Balanced on two pillars in the river Cher, the elegant château was added to by later *châtelaines*. Henri II gave Chenonceau to Diane de Poitiers, his companion for 22 years. Diane built a bridge connecting it to the left bank of the Cher; she also designed a classical park, with fountains fed by a complex irrigation system which still exists. Henri's wife, Catherine de Médicis, bided her time and, on Henri's death, forced Diane to accept Chaumont as poor exchange for Chenonceau. Still, Diane's bed, as if vindicated by history, has been moved into the Chambre des Cinque Reines, room of the five queens. When Flaubert stayed here, he remarked that, "Even empty, Diane de Poitier's canopied bed inspires many palpable realities".

When the sweet taste of revenge

over Diane faded, Catherine also learned to love Chenonceau. She created a cross between a French palace and an Italian villa, with grottoes and fountains, oranges and olives: a patch of Mediterranean colour under a northern sky. Catherine's library and study, tucked into the oldest tower, are preserved exactly as she left them: the ornate ceilings have not been touched since 1521. Her crowning achievement is the elegant gallery that stretches across the river. On her death, Chenonceau passed to Louise de Lorraine, Henri III's widow, who spent the rest of her life in white, the colour of royal mourning. Her black room, under the eaves, is studded with symbolic silver tears.

Before leaving for a boat trip on the Cher, pay your respects to Chenonceau's three great *châtelaines*. In the François I room, look at the portrait of Diane as legendary huntress. Catherine Briçonnet's epitaph appears on a door nearby, 's'il vient à point me souviendra' (if this château is finished, remember me). As for Catherine de Médicis, her memorial is there in stone and water: the cool gallery and Italianate fountains.

After spending at least two hours in Chenonceau, have an early lunch in **Les Gourmandises de Touraine**, just outside the grounds. Try the regional menu, with pork *rillettes*, spicy *andouillettes* and sweet *pruneaux* for dessert. After glancing at the village church, take the D140 to **Tours** and park in Place de la Résistance, close to the Loire. From here, walk to Rue de Commerce and admire the exquisite Renaissance facade of **Hôtel Gouin**, a silk merchant's house tucked away behind this bustling street. Continue along Rue du Commerce to **Place Plumereau**, the restored heart of medieval Tours, and the place for people-watching from an outdoor café. Since this is also the university quarter, these interlocking squares are lively day and night. Amidst the timber-framed houses, admire the carved facade of a lace shop on the corner of the square and Rue du Change.

Once refreshed, walk under a gateway to **St Pierre le Puellier**, a tiny medieval square with sunken Gallo-Roman remains and a Romanesque church converted into a trendy café. From here, a stone gateway leads to **Le Jardin des Chanoines**, a medieval courtyard with houses converted from earlier cloisters. Several of these tiny courtyards off **Rue Briçonnet** reveal twisted brick-and-timber towers, symbols of Tours. **Place des Carmes**, once the rich merchants' quarter, is now a haven of peace, adorned with grand 18th-century mansions. Just west of this gentrified area is the artisans' quarter, centred on **Rue du Petit**

Hôtel Gouin

Place Plumereau

St Martin. This venture is a model of French urban development, with workers housed in renovated buildings in return for practising traditional crafts, from weaving to jewellery-making.

From the artisans' quarter walk along Rue du Grand Marché to Place du Grand Marché, the lively market district, centred on **Les Halles**. On the adjoining Place Gaston-Pailhou, join the market traders for a glass of Chinon wine in Bistrot des Halles or enjoy a choice of 240 beers in the rough and ready Palais de la Bière. From Les Halles, take Rue du Châteauneuf to the quiet square of the same name and look at the Romanesque **Tour Charlemagne**, all that remains of St Martin's original church. Just off the square is the dramatic 19th-century basilica built to contain St Martin's tomb.

From here, walk towards Place Plumereau and take Rue du Commerce east to Rue Nationale. This ugly new quarter, the result of wartime bombing, conceals glorious vestiges of Vieux Tours. An unpromising archway off 34 Rue Nationale leads to the Romanesque church of **St Julien** which contains a wine museum in the former monks' cells as well as the unique **Musée du Compagnonnage**, a collection of old crafts (9–12am, 2–7pm). The enchanting garden has a porticoed chapel, along with a fountain and a Renaissance facade pierced by trees. At night it is magical, with light dancing on the marble fountain.

From here, follow Rue Colbert to the **Cathedral**. The majestic Gothic exterior is enlivened by vivid medieval rose windows and 15th-century cloisters. If you have the energy, walk behind the Cathedral to admire the flying buttresses and appreciate **Tours'** Roman remains. Take the semicircular Rue Général Meunier along the remnants of the Roman arena and return along the walled Rue Manceau, celebrated by Balzac. Virtually next door to the Cathedral is the **Musée des Beaux Arts** (9–12.45, 2–6pm). This former bishops' palace in classical grounds provides a fine display case for portraits and regional landscapes.

The Cathedral

The Petit St Martin area

Most restaurants are sandwiched between the leaning towers of Rue de la Rôtisserie and busy Rue du Commerce. For light meals, Tours *crêperies* are excellent, particularly **Le Royal Crêp'** (22 Rue de la Rôtisserie), opposite a piano bar. To escape the crowds, dine in unostentatious Rue Colbert. **Au Coeur Navré** (16 Rue Colbert) is a medieval inn adjoining a secret passage of the same name. In the 13th century, this was where the condemned passed on their way to being hanged in **Place Foire-le-Roi**. The aroma of *coq au vin* cannot quite dispel one's unease. But risk this 'passage of the broken-hearted' to admire the illuminated fountain and Hôtel Babou, a sculpted Renaissance mansion on the riverside square.

After dinner, walk along **Rue Colbert** and admire the medieval buildings, including number 39, where Joan of Arc is supposed to have tried on her armour; local cynics say Joan of Arc seems to have stayed all over the place. From here, return to the **Plumereau quarter** for ice cream or liqueurs.

Culturally, Tours is the richest of the Loire towns. On summer evenings, the streets echo with competing sounds, from live jazz to Chopin's greatest hits tinkling from a piano bar. Stay out late and savour the liveliness of the old quarter. Yet even in the height of summer you can slip into the tiny squares behind Place Plumereau and find yourself alone with the ghosts of monks.

Staying In and Dining Out

$$$$ Luxury
$$$ Expensive
$$ Moderate
$ Inexpensive

Chenonceaux

HOTEL DU BON LABOUREUR
*6 Rue du Dr Bretonneau,
37150 Chenonceaux.
Tel: 47 23 90 02.*
Popular inn with pool, so book. Candlelit dinners on terrace. Noted restaurant: try the duck in Chinon wine; stuffed sole. *$$$.*

HOSTEL DU ROY
*9 Rue du Dr Bretonneau,
37150 Chenonceaux.
Tel: 47 23 90 17.*
Converted farmhouse hotel/restaurant in the village. Rustic decor, terrace, garden. Friendly. Good wine list. *$$.*

Tours (and just outside)

CHATEAU D'ARTIGNY
*Rue d'Azay-le-Rideau,
Montbazon, 37250 Veigné.
Tel: 47 26 24 24.*
Imposing classical mansion in vast grounds. Pool. Formal, Empire style, gourmet restaurant. 8km (5 miles) south of Tours. *$$$$.*

MANOIR DU GRAND MARTIGNY
*Vallières, 37230 Fondettes.
Tel: 47 42 29 87.*
Peaceful hotel in manor house, 5km (3 miles) west of Tours. *$$$.*

LE MOULIN FLEURI
*Route du Ripault,
Montbazon, 37250 Veigné.
Tel: 47 26 01 12.*
In 16th-century mill on river Indre, 8km (5 miles) south of Tours. Classic cuisine in rustic dining room. *$$.*

HOTEL DU THÉATRE
*57 Rue de la Scellerie, 37000 Tours.
Tel: 47 05 31 29.*
Charming, old-fashioned hotel in centre of Old Tours. *$$.*

BARDET
*57 Rue Groison, 37000 Tours.
Tel: 47 41 41 11.*
The most celebrated gourmet restaurant in the Loire. *$$$$.*

Vouvray

LES HAUTES ROCHES
*86 Quai de la Loire,
Rochecorbon, 37210 Vouvray.
Tel: 47 52 88 88.*
Luxurious bedrooms in converted troglodyte caves overlooking the river. Terraced restaurant. *$$$$.*

CHATEAU DE JALLANGES
*Vallée de Vaugondy,
37210 Vernou-sur-Brenne.
Tel: 47 52 01 71.*
Family-run Renaissance château in a village near Vouvray. Medieval cuisine on request! *$$$.*

MADAME FORTIER,
LE CHENE MORIER, (B&B)
*37210 Vouvray.
Tel: 47 52 78 83.*
Comfortable rooms in modern, secluded house overlooking valley. Pool on site. Popular so book. *$.*

MONSIEUR BELLANGER,
AUBERGE DE LA CAVE MARTIN
*66, La Vallée Coquette,
37210 Vouvray.
Tel: 47 52 62 18 or 47 56 11 29.*
A working farm in vineyards: meals with the family. *Foie gras* and grills on the terrace. Book. *$.*

Tours → Chinon
DAY 4

Garden of France

This full-day excursion visits Villandry's Renaissance gardens as well as Azay-le-Rideau and Ussé, the region's most romantic chateaux, before dinner in cosy Chinon.

From Tours, take the D7 to the village of Savonnières and descend into the **Grottes Pétrifiantes** (9am–7pm). These prehistoric caves contain strange formations in a watery setting. But if you prefer heights to depths, visit the Romanesque village church and climb the steep steps behind, leading to sweeping views. From here, follow the river Cher to **Villandry** (9am–6pm), the Loire's loveliest gardens. The château itself is a paler version of Villesavin so restrict your visit to the glorious tiered gardens.

Villandry's gardens were restored to their Renaissance splendour by Joachim Carvallo. Robert Carvallo has followed in his grandfather's footsteps, somewhat at the expense of his family: 'the gardens cost my children a good education and caused my wife a nervous breakdown'. Luckily, the result is breathtaking, whatever the season. The ornamental, water and kitchen gardens are comple-

Villandry's Renaissance gardens

Villandry

mentary, replanted twice a year so that the plants, hues and design of the spring and summer gardens differ. The spring patchwork bursts with pansies, tulips and salad vegetables; late summer celebrates fruit crops, dahlias, petunias and blue ornamental cabbages. Of the three gardens, the kitchen garden rules, with its nine geometrical beds and honeysuckle-covered bowers.

Gardens like these were first created by medieval monks whose cultivation was functional but who also cherished spiritual symbols, with red roses representing eternal love. In the Renaissance ornamental terraces vied with purely decorative vegetable gardens. The plants were also prized for their medicinal properties: strawberries acted as a mild diuretic, cabbage helped to cure hangovers, pimento to aid digestion, and lemons to prolong life. There are signs to explain the history and symbolism of each plant: the marrow, imported from Italy in the 16th century, represents fertility; parsley symbolises sexual and spiritual corruption; strawberries, introduced from South America, are the legendary fruit of the gods.

From the highest terrace, admire the *jardins d'amour*, representing romantic, passionate, tragic and fickle love. While tragic love is portrayed by crossed swords, fickle love takes the form of treacherous love letters and yellow flowers, the colour of betrayal. Before leaving, look at the swans and snow geese on the ornamental lake and the huge carp in the moats. Also breathe in the pungent herb garden, the tiger roses by the box-wood hedges and the shady lines of linden trees.

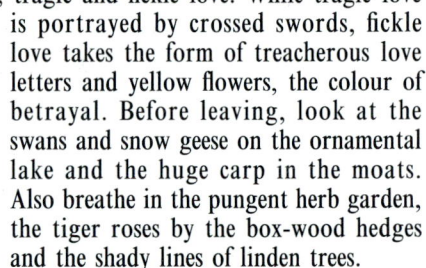

From here, take the D39 across country to **Azay-le-Rideau** (9am–6.30pm). Like Chenonceau, Azay was a pleasure palace, lived in during fine weather and abandoned to the mists in winter. A tree-lined drive reveals an intricate system of moats and weirs. Although built on an island of piles, Azay appears to float on the waters of the Indre. It is the most beguiling and feminine of all Loire chateaux. Created by Philippa Lesbaye,

Azay-le-Rideau

the wife of François I's financier, this Renaissance dream bears her motto: 'un seul désir', a sign of her passion for Azay. But after Philippa's husband was accused of embezzlement, François seized Azay and his salamander symbol now climbs over the facade.

The guided tour of the chateau is illuminating about Azay's domestic details. In Renaissance times, privileged guests slept on cushions around the host's bed: as a reward for telling racy bedtime stories, guests were fed sweetmeats. Less-favoured visitors reclined on chests or slept seven to a bed. Servants slept on the creaking floorboards at their master's feet. Living in a Renaissance film set meant never going to bed alone. The subdued decor, secret cabinets and family portraits all add to the intimate atmosphere. Equally entrancing is Azay's amateurish but poetic *son et lumière*, when, the spotlight is on the dreamy architecture and the Renaissance-style boats gliding across the water lilies.

Renaissance eating took place anywhere: the notion of a dining room only emerged in the 18th century. If you want a proper dining room, choose *rillettes, andouillettes* and *rosé* in Azay's **Le Grand Monarque** (3 Place de la République, Tel: 47 45 40 08). For a lighter lunch, consider *crêpes* in Azay. Alternatively, enjoy a picnic at Bréhémont, a former port and hemp-growing village. As for accommodation, Azay and Chinon are lively touring bases but for peace and quiet, choose Bréhémont or a wine estate in Huismes.

From Azay, take the D17 along the banks of the Indre to the **Château d'Ussé** (9–12am, 2–7pm). Framed by the forest of Chinon, this fairytale cluster of white towers was the inspiration for Sleeping Beauty. But Ussé's owner, the Marquis de Blacas, is no Prince Charming. This international lawyer has turned his entrepreuneurial eye to his childhood home. Complaining about this 'bottomless pit', the affable marquis shrewdly appreciates that 'every visitor represents one new slate'. At weekends, he can be found doing carpentry jobs or putting promotional leaflets on car windscreens.

Sadly, the brusque guide is of the hope-you-enjoyed-your-flight school. Nor is an enchanting setting matched by the sunless and slightly dingy interior. Even so, unlike in many Loire châteaux, the musty furnishings are original. Look out for a Florentine cabinet with 49 secret drawers in an antechamber. In the parapet rooms, the Sleeping Beauty *tableaux* are comically garish, as are Ussé's

Château d'Ussé

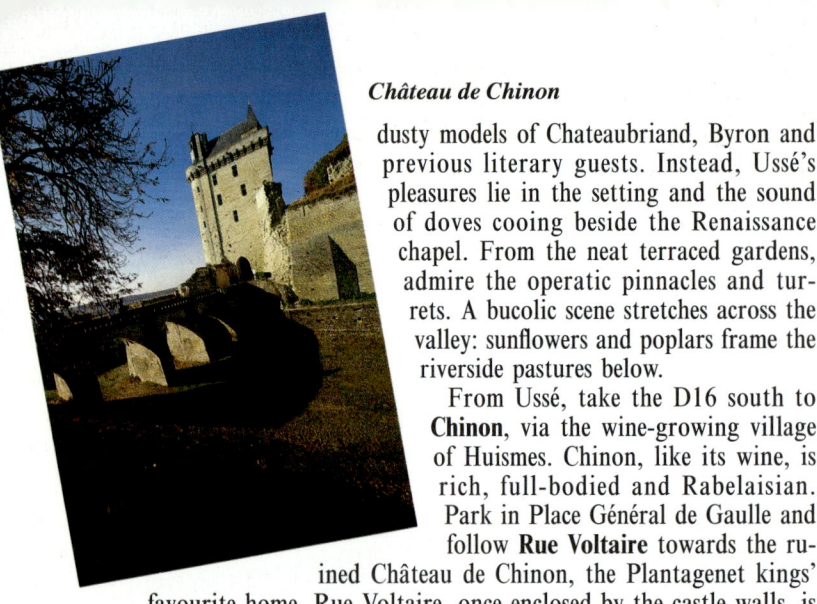

Château de Chinon

dusty models of Chateaubriand, Byron and previous literary guests. Instead, Ussé's pleasures lie in the setting and the sound of doves cooing beside the Renaissance chapel. From the neat terraced gardens, admire the operatic pinnacles and turrets. A bucolic scene stretches across the valley: sunflowers and poplars frame the riverside pastures below.

From Ussé, take the D16 south to **Chinon**, via the wine-growing village of Huismes. Chinon, like its wine, is rich, full-bodied and Rabelaisian. Park in Place Général de Gaulle and follow **Rue Voltaire** towards the ruined Château de Chinon, the Plantagenet kings' favourite home. Rue Voltaire, once enclosed by the castle walls, is a cross-section of *Chinonais* history. Medieval timber-framed houses lead to Renaissance *tuffeau* stone ones. At the Grand Carroi, admire the Maison Rouge, with its red-brick herringbone design. Next door is the turreted stone mansion where, in 1199, Richard the Lionheart died of wounds received at Chalus. Now a charming town museum, it is surrounded by a rose garden.

Further along Rue Voltaire are sculpted Renaissance *hôtels* and classical stone mansions with elegant courtyards. The grandest is number 48, the Hôtel du Gouvernement, with its double staircase, loggia and views of the castle beyond. Further on is the turreted **Hostellerie Gargantua**, once a tribunal where Rabelais' father used to plead. This inn serves suitably gargantuan portions of leek and chicken *cassoulet* in Chinon wine. A Rabelaisian day must end in a feast. (To explore Chinon further, follow Option 6.)

Tapestry in Ussé

The landscape at Pont de Ruan inspired Balzac

Option 5: Balzac Country

This half-day trip visits the valley of the river Indre, the landscape celebrated by Balzac. After the Balzac museum in Saché it goes on to Villaines, a weaving village near Azay.

'Do not ask me why I love Touraine: I love it as an artist loves art.' Honoré de Balzac's praise of Touraine was heart-felt: his years here represent the most creative period of his life. In print, he depicted the foibles of the landed gentry against a pastoral idyll. In reality, he drank in the *douceur de vivre* of Touraine. Balzac particularly loved the Indre valley, with its pale gold poplars, rushes and lilies. This stretch of river was the setting for a love scene in *Le Lys dans la Vallée*. This was 'the vale of love . . . a long ribbon of water streaming in the sun between two green banks'.

From Azay-le-Rideau follow the D84 east towards Pont de Ruan, along the north bank of the river Indre. This rural drive meanders past lush meadows, strawberry beds and sunflowers. After passing a cluster of manor houses and a hamlet, the narrow river winds on to **Pont de Ruan**. From the bridge, there are views of ruined water mills beside rushing weirs and weeping willows. Balzac used to walk here from Tours and described 'three mills set among islands gracefully divided and crowned with clusters of trees amidst a water-meadow'.

From here, cross to the south bank of the Indre and take the D17 west to the **Château de Saché** (9–12am, 2–6pm). Balzac's relationship with Saché verges on the incestuous. Saché, a fine 16th-century manor house, belonged to family friends – to his mother's former lover, to be precise. Given that Saché's owner Monsieur de Margonne also fathered Balzac's brother, it was natural for him to treat Honoré as a second son. Balzac visited often between 1823–37,

Château de Saché, where Balzac was a frequent visitor

in retreat from Parisian creditors. There he pronounced himself 'as happy as a monk in a monastery', and set about writing *Le Père Goriot* and *Le Lys dans la Vallée*, works inspired by his beloved Touraine.

Saché's austere dining room is covered with the wallpaper Balzac loved. The formal sitting room was where the writer mimed scenes from work in progress. The house bursts with manuscripts and portraits of Balzac and his many mistresses. He wrote in a tiny bed with a view of the Indre valley from the window. In this bedroom Balzac literally burnt the midnight oil, living on fruit tarts, litres of coffee and little sleep. For something more substantial than a fruit tart, call in at **L'Auberge du 12e Siècle** (Tel: 47 26 88 77). Saché's charming rustic inn is the place to enjoy grilled fish while appreciating Balzac's taste in landscape.

From Saché, drive south to **Villaines-les-Rochers**, a village carved out of a rocky hillside. Villaines is devoted to the old craft of wickerwork. **Vannerie des Villaines** (9–12am, 2–6pm) is a co-operative set up 150 years ago by the *curé* to help his flock. Eighty families carry out the work, which is all done by hand, from soaking and binding to stripping and shaping, producing baskets, trays, mats and bird cages. After looking at the cluster of troglodyte dwellings, have a glass of local wine in **Le Bellevue** (22 Rue du Chillou, Tel: 47 45 43 68). The aroma of sizzling fish is in the air but one's eye falls upon the wickerwork decorations. Expect to return to Azay-le-Rideau with an appealing but useless wicker basket on your arm.

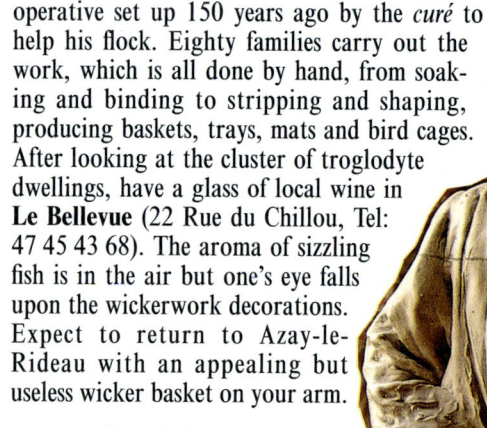

Statue of Balzac at Saché

Option 6: Chinon and Bourgueil

This half-day excursion visits Chinon's wine museum before sampling the competing Chinon and Bourgueil red wines.

To make this into a full-day trip, visit Chinon's château and churches or consider a river cruise. From Rue Voltaire, take any path to the quays on the river Vienne and admire the Renaissance facades. The quays were formed when the castle ramparts were demolished. If the idea of a river cruise appeals, call in at the **tourist office** (12 Rue Voltaire, Tel: 47 93 17 85). The same applies if you wish to see church interiors. Romanesque Saint-Mexme is being restored but try to see the troglodyte St Radegonde.

Rumbustious Rabelais is Chinon's most famous son. From Rue Voltaire, take the medieval **Impasse des Caves-Peintes** for a glimpse of the wine confraternity Rabelais knew well. Called Les Bons Entonneurs Rabelaisiens, this bacchic gathering today boasts celebrities such as Gérard Depardieu and Elisabeth Taylor among its members. The red-robed members meet in these frescoed caverns for singing, feasting and much downing of Chinon.

The best red Chinon and Bourgueil resemble rich Bordeaux. According to wine expert Oz Clarke, these full-bodied reds have an unforgettable personality, 'strangely earthy, dry and sharp-edged, yet with a beautiful, almost searing laser-beam of blackcurrant and wild strawberry fruit'. Chinon, produced from the Cabernet Franc grape, grows on both sides of the river Vienne. Chinon from the slopes matures well while the wine from the plains tends to be lighter, fruitier and drunk younger. Both go well with meat but are perfect with poultry, particularly *coq au vin*, with Chinon used in the sauce and drunk with the meal.

Musée Animé du Vin (12 Rue Voltaire, 10–12am, 2–6pm) is a light-hearted homage to the fabled red wine. Set in vaulted caves, the museum uses creaking automated models to show the stages of wine-making, from pressing to cask-making. One room includes a comical 'Rabelaisian' dialogue between two elderly Chinon folks. Rabelais' words of wisdom include: 'Beuvez toujours, ne mourez jamais' (Drink, and you'll live forever). Nearby, on Quai Pasteur, **Caves de Monplaisir** (8–12am, 2–6pm) are wine cellars lurking in the château dungeons.

For a wine-tasting in a more scenic setting, drive 2km (1¼ miles) north along the D16 to **Château de la Grille** (Tel: 47 93 01 95). The cellars have been carved out of the *tuffeau* stone under the 15th-century château. Albert Gosset, the owner, recommends the violet-scented 1985, the fruity 1987 and, if you can wait five years to drink it, the exceptional 1989 vintage. The bottles themselves are lovely replicas of 18th-century Chinon flasks. From here, drive to **Bourgueil**.

Jules Romain called Chinon 'wine for intellectuals'. If so, Bourgueil must be 'wine for monks', originally produced by the Benedictines. The monks have mostly gone but the abbey remains, as do the vineyards. Visit the **Abbaye de Bourgueil** (2–6pm) to see the gardens, monks' cells, a fine tithe barn and a glorious vaulted staircase. If you are lucky, a classical concert may be staged in the evening.

Afterwards, combine religion and red wine with a visit to **Clos de l'Abbaye** (Tel: 47 97 76 30, 2.30–7pm), a wine estate run by nuns. Expect smokey, aromatic wines which, like Chinon, improve with age. Also in Bourgueil is **Cave de la Dive Bouteille** (10–12.30am, 2.30–7.30pm), an atmospheric wine museum in vaulted cellars. After a *dégustation*, sample their local dishes. Fruity Bourgueil from the plains is excellent with white meat, grills and roasts, while wine from the slopes is best with red meat, *coq au vin* and cheeses.

St-Nicolas-de-Bourgueil, grown nearby, is a lighter version of Bourgueil. The best-known producer is **Joel Taluau** (Chevrette, St-Nicolas-de-Bourgueil, Tel: 47 97 78 79). His 1988 vintage has the perfect peppery note and scent of raspberries. Alternatively, visit the welcoming Amiraux family at **Clos des Quarterons** (St-Nicolas-de-Bourgueil, Tel: 47 97 75 25). Theirs is a traditional wine estate producing fruity, spicy wines.

These border wines, grown on the edges of Anjou and west Touraine, are produced by great *bons vivants*. The hospitality of this region is legendary and *vignerons* are friendlier and less formal than elsewhere in the Loire. Expect to be wished 'Un bon séjour en Rabelaisie,' a happy stay in Rabelais' region. As Rabelais said in an old French word not unlike its modern English equivalent: 'Trinc!'

Renaissance grape treading

Staying In and Dining Out

$$$$ Luxury
$$$ Expensive
$$ Moderate
$ Inexpensive

Azay-Le-Rideau

MANOIR DE LA RÉMONIERE (B&B)
Cheille, 37190 Azay-le-Rideau.
Tel: 47 45 24 88.
Restored hunting lodge outside Azay on the D17, Rooms $$$. Meals $$.

BERNADETTE WILMANN,
LE CLOS PHILIPPA (B&B)
10 Rue Pineau, 37190 Azay-le-Rideau.
Tel: 47 45 26 49 or 47 48 37 13.
Charming 18th-century family house near the château. $$.

LES GROTTES
23 Ter, Rue Pineau,
37190 Azay-le-Rideau.
Tel: 47 45 21 04.
'Troglodyte' restaurant. Specialities from Touraine. $$.

AU RELAIS DU CHATEAU
5 Rue du Pineau, Azay-le-Rideau.
Tel: 47 45 30 42.
Crêperie, pizzeria and grill. $.

Chinon

CHATEAU DE MARÇAY
37500 Marçay.
Tel: 47 93 03 47.
Château hotel with gourmet restaurant south of Chinon (D116). Pool, tennis courts, terrace. $$$$.

HOSTELLERIE GARGANTUA
73 Rue Voltaire, 37500 Chinon.
Tel: 47 93 04 71.
A 15th-century courthouse with noted cuisine. At weekends, dinner is served by staff in medieval costumes. $$$.

HOTEL DIDEROT
4 Rue Buffon, 37500 Chinon.
Tel: 47 93 18 87.
Charming town mansion run by helpful Cypriot couple. $$.

LE PLAISIR GOURMAND
2 Rue Parmentier, 37500 Chinon.
Tel: 47 93 20 48.
Gourmet restaurant in Renaissance town house. Book. $$$.

LES ANNÉES 30
78 Rue Voltaire, 37500 Chinon.
Tel; 47 93 37 18.
1930s restaurant with regional menu: pike; *rillons*. $$.

Langeais/Usse/Villandry

LE CASTEL DE BRAY ET MONTS
Place de l'Eglise, Bréhémont,
37130 Langeais.
Tel: 47 96 70 47.
18th-century waterside manor with elegant cuisine (and cookery courses) south-west of Langeais (D16). $$–$$$.

ANGELA & DEREK SMITH,
LES BRUNETS (B&B)
Bréhémont, 37130 Langeais.
Tel: 47 96 55 81.
Welcoming English family in attractive, cosy farmhouse. $.

MICHEL SALLES,
MANOIR DE FONCHER (B&B)
37510 Villandry.
Tel: 47 50 02 40.
Period manor overlooking Chateau de Villandry. English spoken. Meals available there. Popular so book. $$$.

DOMAINE DE LA GIRAUDIERE
Route de Druye, 37510 Villandry.
Tel: 47 50 08 60.
Rustic farmhouse restaurant: quiche; omelettes; stuffed tomatoes; pâté; cheeses (from own goats). $.

Chinon → Saumur

DAY 5

Spirit of Anjou

This full-day excursion begins in La Devinière, Rabelais' home, before visiting Fontevraud Abbey and continuing downriver to Saumur, a route rich in churches and troglodyte caves.

La Devinière

From Chinon, take the D751 and turn left at the sign for **La Devinière** (10am–7pm). Rabelais' birthplace is an erstwhile farm surrounded by the rolling countryside he described so vividly. The ground floor is only for scholars but the upstairs conveys enough rough intimacy to conjure up Rabelais' presence. A portrait by Matisse adorns the walls, as do fruity Rabelaisian sayings on wine and friendship. The underground stables suggest the earthiness of a man who could celebrate Gargantua's mare drowning an army in her piss. In the garden, notice the Gargantuan model and the Rabelaisian map of the world. The region's abbeys, châteaux, peasants and bottles all roared into his rumbustious prose.

From here, continue along the D751 to **Candes-St-Martin**, a bleached stone village at the meeting of the Loire and Vienne. St Martin died here in AD397 and a Romanesque church was built on the spot. Legend has it that on his death in November all of Touraine burst into bloom; a late summer has since been known as 'L'été de St Martin'. The church has Angevin vaulting, sculpted capitals and a porch adorned with Biblical scenes, notably a Last Judgment frieze. If you are feeling energetic, climb the cobbled

Stained glass in Candes-St-Martin

path to a panoramic view devoid of villages: below is a timeless, marshy landscape with Chinon's stark nuclear reactor the sole anachronism.

At Monsoreau, take the D147 south to **Fontevraud L'Abbaye** and park in Avenue du II Novembre. Walk along an avenue of lindens to **St Michel**, an early Plantagenet church hemmed in by a delicate wooden porch and pots of geraniums. Inside, notice the Angevin vaulting, Gothic statuary, garish altar piece and the reliquaries originally housed in the abbey. In the same avenue, admire the **Chapelle St Catherine**, a medieval *monument des morts*, originally part of the nuns' cemetery but now the tourist office.

Fontevraud, France's most royal abbey, was founded by Robert d'Arbissel in 1047. Although Benedictine, the abbey had a strong Marian cult and was mixed-sex, with a nunnery and a monastery. Even more radical was the founder's decision to entrust Fontevraud to an abbess. Given that the post included supervision of 100 dependent abbeys, it soon became a royal appointment bestowed upon a queen or princess. As well as the monastery and nunnery, the abbey housed a leper colony, a hospital and a home for repentant prostitutes. From 1804 to 1963 the abbey was used as a prison, with inmates forced to make mother of pearl buttons. Jean Genet, once a prisoner here, was inspired by visions of debauched monks and prostitutes and used the setting for his plays.

Much remains intact, from the sober abbey church to the chapter house, cloisters and refectory. In the church are the tombstone effigies of the Plantagenets: Henry II, Richard the Lionheart and Eleanor of Aquitaine, with a book in her hands. Nor should we forget sly Isabelle d'Angoulême whose husband, King John, married her by force; she fed him poisoned peaches and was soon a widow. The British fretfully claim the effigies for Westminster Abbey but the French are adamant: these are French epic heroes.

With their ingenious chimneys, the Romanesque abbey kitchens resemble a folly or dovecote. Inside, their austere beauty is rem-

Fontevraud Abbey

iniscent of a chapel, not of a factory that once produced 2,000 smoked fish daily, not to mention the roasts. If this stirs the appetite, consider lunching here. (See *Staying In and Dining Out* below.) From Fontevraud, return to **Monsoreau** and gaze at the towering château, which was once only accessible by river. Consider a drink or late lunch in a former chapterhouse below the château (Le Chapitre, Quai A Dumas, Tel: 41 51 75 33). The troglodyte-encrusted slopes between here and **Turquant** are dotted with mills and underground farms.

Turquant knows that troglodytes are the secret of success: apart from cave-like homes, wine cellars and mushrooom farms, look out for an underground Vietnamese restaurant and, most ingenious of all, a dried apple farm. **Troglo Tap** (10–12am, 2.30–6.30pm) has revived the old craft of roasting apples, reconstituting them with stewed wine and selling them to the British Royal Navy and other traditional enemies. Known as *pommes tapées*, these are an experience best confined to a long voyage.

Just downriver is **Saumur**, a town celebrated for its château and sparkling wines, cavalry and churches. Saumur's stone mansions recall its 17th-century heyday, when the city vied with Angers as the intellectual capital of Anjou. Henri III made Saumur a Protestant stronghold, creating a garrison and establishing a Protestant Academy. During this period, fine town houses were built for the influx of rich foreign merchants and scholars. As a pilgrimage centre, Saumur also did a roaring trade in religious objects. It remained a bastion of Protestantism until 1685 when the Catholic revival saw the desecration of Saumur's churches.

Park on **Place de la République** and follow this leisurely stroll to the château itself. Begin by the **Loire** and look out for flat-bottomed boats. Known as *gabelles*, these barges used to carry silk to

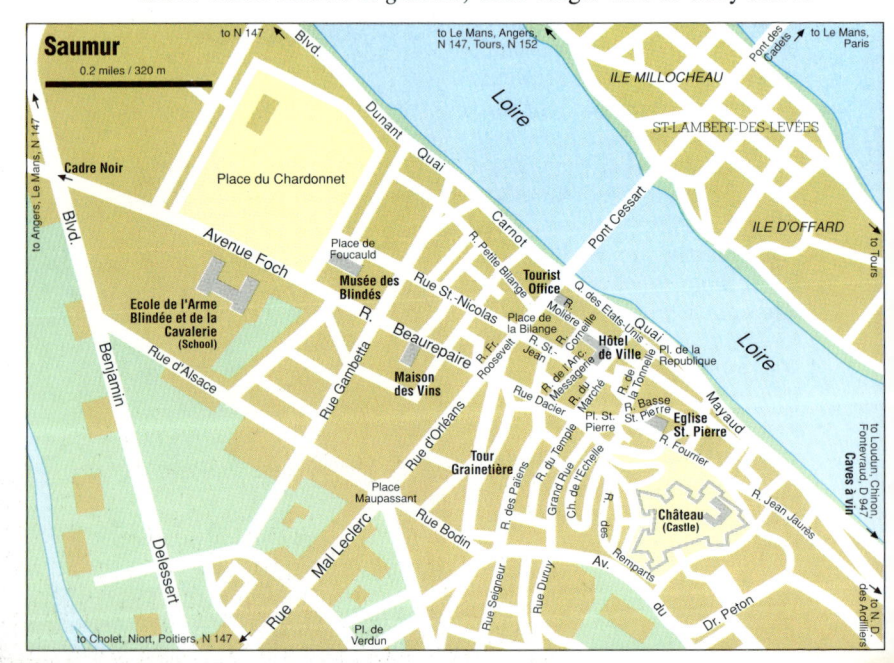

Saumur, bastion of Protestantism

London but now carry the odd tourist to the island and the opposite bank. Once a forsaken marsh, this is now the showroom for Saumur's controversial modern architecture. Saumur's renovation projects are no less controversial and a case in point is the turreted **Hôtel de Ville**, just across the square. Walk through the arch to the inner courtyard and compare the restored and unrestored sections of the facade.

From here, walk down Rue Corneille to the Plantagenet St Jean church before turning right into Rue de l'Ancienne Messagerie. The Fontevraud abbesses lived at number 6, choosing to be near the royal court and thus benefit from ecclesiastical taxes. At end of the street (33 Rue Dacier) is the stone house King René preferred to his draughty château. Continue down Rue des Paiens, a corruption of 'pagans', a term for people baptised late in life. See number 2, lived in by Mark Duncan, a Calvinist philosopher. Nearby is the **Tour Grenetière**, a medieval prison with an over-restored tower. At the end of the road, take Rue du Temple, named after two Protestant churches. After passing turreted mansions, turn into the Grand Rue and notice the wine cellars, a reminder that Saumur was once a troglodyte town.

Saumur is predominantly a city of stone but **Place St Pierre**, further on, is a sweet square with half-timbered houses. The church has a Jesuit-style facade and bears the motto *plus robuste qu'avant* (stronger than before) as a reminder of its earlier death by fire. From here, climb the quaint **Montée du Fort** to a delicious house, **Maison des Compagnons**, the setting for Balzac's *Eugénie Grandet*. Notice the gallery and the gargoyle-encrusted fountain before looking down over St Pierre's belfry and gazing up at the **château** (9am–6.30pm).

The fairytale château of Saumur echoes the miniature in *Les Très Riches Heures du Duc de Berry*: four towers

Cave houses

survey the city and the river. It was built in the 15th century by Bon Roi René who lived up to his name. However, the château and its contents are disconnected: ceramics occupy the lower floors while, under the eaves, the horse reigns supreme, with saddles and equestrian sculptures everywhere. The obligatory guided tour is perfunctory but visitors may canter around the grounds alone.

From here, walk along Rue J Jaurès to **Notre Dame des Ardilliers**, a classical church on the Compostela pilgrimage route. Then leave the river for a walk around the ramparts and to **Notre Dame de Nantilly**. The church boasts a Romanesque nave and capitals sculpted with griffins and flowers, a prelude to Cunault (Option 9).

For dinner, Saumur is a delight (see *Staying In and Dining Out*). Since Saumur is France's foremost producer of *champignons de Paris*, mushrooms are *de rigueur*. Afterwards, consider an equestrian show by the Cadre Noir or an atmospheric torchlit tour of the **Château de Montreuil-Bellay** (see Option 8). The tourist office in the Place de la Bilange should have information (Tel: 41 51 03 06).

Option 7: The Troglodyte Trail

This half or full-day excursion visits the plains south of Saumur and discovers a complete underground world.

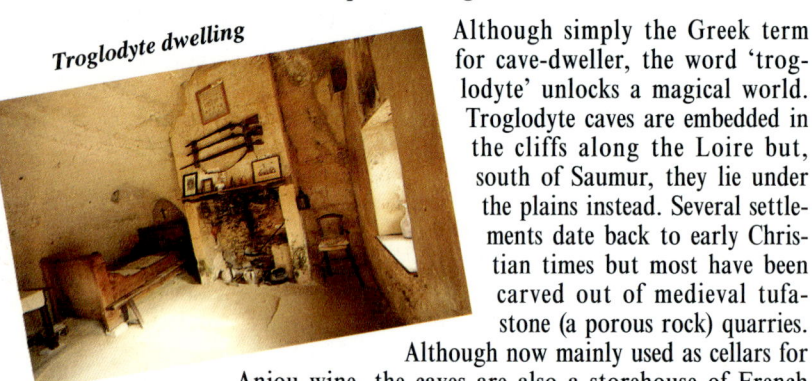

Troglodyte dwelling

Although simply the Greek term for cave-dweller, the word 'troglodyte' unlocks a magical world. Troglodyte caves are embedded in the cliffs along the Loire but, south of Saumur, they lie under the plains instead. Several settlements date back to early Christian times but most have been carved out of medieval tufastone (a porous rock) quarries. Although now mainly used as cellars for Anjou wine, the caves are also a storehouse of French history. In the Saumur region, cave dwellings were common until 1914 and, still today, form troglodyte farms and second homes. Given their versatility and tourist appeal, the caves are increasingly being turned into mushroom farms and rustic restaurants, not to mention an underground zoo, discotheque, theatre and hotel.

From Saumur, take the D960 to Doué-la-Fontaine and follow signs to **Les Arènes** (10–12am, 2–5pm). This amphitheatre, in use since medieval times, covers a warren of tunnels built out of *falun*, the fossil-encrusted local stone. However, the town is best known as *La Cité des Roses*. **Le Jardin des Roses** in Parc Foulon boasts 500 varieties and is at its most magnificent in July. Glance at the mound-like troglodyte dwellings on **Rue des Perrières** before driving to Forges, 4km (2½ miles) east of Doué on the D214.

Here, just across the sunflower plains lurks the underground hamlet of **La Fosse** (10–12.30am, 2–6pm). These 17th-century farms are still lived in and conceal a buried grain silo, a hemp dryer and an ingenious two-tier well. After being shown round by the residents, take the D177 to Louresse-Rochemenier and its **Village Troglodytique** (9.30–12am, 2–7pm). This settlement, three times the size of the village above ground, dates from the Middle Ages. The farmers first dug out a courtyard and sold the stone, thus covering the costs of building. The farms, grouped around the sunken courtyard, present a self-sufficient community with stables, cellars, bedrooms, a village hall and even a 13th-century chapel. The rooms paint an austere picture of life before World War I, from damp bedrooms to windows sealed by oiled paper. One has to admire the ingenuity of the pine resin candles, wine chutes, walnut presses, manure pallets and dog-drawn carts. Afterwards, enjoy a rustic meal at the local **Caves de la Genevraie** (Tel: 41 59 04 06). Sample *repas fouaces, crêpes* from underground ovens.

From here, follow signs to Dénézé-sous-Doué and La Caverne Sculpté (10am–7pm). This 16th-century cave was decorated by stonemasons who defied authority by meeting in secret here. Exceptionally for the times, Protestants, Catholics and Jews formed a close-knit group and expressed their frustrations by carving a witty commentary on the walls. This political satire has often been mistaken for sacrilege and the caves were hidden until recently by horrified local priests. The carvings depict 16th century taste, from the court fashions for bare-breasted gowns to long johns, introduced from Italy by Catherine de Médicis. See these enigmatic sculptures now because poor atmospheric conditions are fast destroying them. In summer there are candle-lit concerts in the caves (Tel: 41 59

15 40). Near Saumur is the **Musée du Champignon** (Tel: 41 50 31 55) a mushroom museum in St Hilaire-St-Florent. Watch sparkling wine being made in the cellars (see Option 9). Doué-la-Fontaine has a **troglodyte zoo** in a quarry (9am–7pm; Tel: 41 59 18 58).

For traditional troglodyte fare, try **Les Caves de Marson** (Tel: 41 50 50 05), a cave-restaurant in Rou-Marson serving *fouées*, crêpes stuffed with beans, cheese and *rillettes*. Turquant offers an exotic underground experience: Vietnamese cuisine in **Le Mandarin** (Tel: 41 38 10 28). There may be a concert in **La Boutinière** (Tel: 41 59 79 33), a troglodyte information centre 5km (3 miles) from Doué. End the day in true caveman-style in **Le Tar'tuff Discothèque** (Tel: 41 59 27 78) in Meigné-sous-Doué.

Option 8: Montreuil-Bellay

This excursion explores the historic town and castle of Montreuil-Bellay, a riverside escape from the crowds.

Montreuil-Bellay, 18km (11¼ miles) south of Saumur, is an excellent base for touring Anjou and a gracious town in its own right, with stylish mansions, noted cuisine and riverside walks. Picnic on a tiny island on the river Thouet, or hire a canoe and float past tumbledown mills, willows, lilies, herons and kingfishers. There is culture aplenty too. The jewel is the **Château** (10–12am, 2–6pm), ideally seen on a romantic torchlit visit.

This Chinese puzzle of a château has 13 interlocking towers and a rich Plantagenet heritage. In Renaissance times the moats were filled in and the medieval fort became a pleasure palace with jousting and falcon-hunting. The medieval flavour of the fortress remains in the barbican, ramparts, towers and vaulted kitchens. But once across the second drawbridge, the impression is of a civilised stately home. It has been home to the Grandmaison family for generations and the present owner is, like his grandfather, a Member of Parliament for the region. The vaulted medieval kitchen, reminiscent of Fontevraud's, is unrestored and still in use. The homely feel is echoed by the family photos, battered copper pots, the smell of jam and the sound of music.

Music is important to Montreuil and is played during the spirited guided tour. The 18th-century music room is still used for family concerts while the Gothic chapel contains faded frescoes of musical angels. According to the housekeeper-guide, 18th-century preachers gave such long sermons that women resorted to chamber pots, concealed in their skirts. As for high jinx, one Aubusson tapestry portrays *le jeu de la main chaude*, an erotic game in which blindfolded gentlemen had to publicly identify their mistresses by placing a 'hot hand' up their dresses. The success rate was extremely low.

Ancient wine cellars run the whole length of the château and are impressive in their size and history. In 1904 the Baron de Grandmaison founded a curious wine confraternity in these vaults. Known as Les Sacavins, their initiation test involved wine-guzzling followed by a climb backwards up the twisting staircase without touching the walls. At the same time, the initiate had to recite a Rabelaisian oath: 'Lorsque mon verre est plein, je le vide, lorsqu'il est vide, je le plains' (If my glass is empty I'll refill it, if it's empty, I'll complain). Since this wine brotherhood is second only to Burgundy's Tastevin in prestige, the test must be easier than it sounds. Before leaving, admire the rose-covered towers in the garden and consider a wine-tasting with the old retainers.

Artist's impression

Certainly have a drink on the **Place du Marché**, the main square, or, for a tasty picnic, pop in to Hatton Traiteur on the same square. For *rillauds, boudin de brochet* (pike *pâté*) and a range of menus, try the **Splendid** (Tel: 41 52 30 21). **Hostellerie St Jean** (Tel: 41 52 30 41) offers gourmet cuisine. However, on a hot day, choose the place with the coolest setting: **Auberge des Isles** (Tel: 41 52 30 63) borders the river and offers *crêpes* and salads, *andouillette* or steaks. If the waterside beckons, choose a spot near the priory to picnic on goat's cheese and local apple-scented white wine.

If you feel like **canoeing** in the direction of Saumur, make arrangements via Montreuil tourist office (Tel: 41 52 32 39). This is the perfect town for children: apart from canoe rides and swimming, there is an **aquarium** (2.30–6.30pm). Alternatively, stroll beside the river, looking at the park, the remains of the Nobis priory,

Château at Montreuil-Bellay

and, further along Rue du Boelle, a miller's house and a city gate.

The **town centre** is compact yet rich in walled mansions and churches. Begin with the Gothic church concealed within the medieval ramparts. Then walk along Rue du Dr Gaudriez to Place des Augustins. This enclosed square is home to a tiny 15th-century chapel and a restored monastic church. Just around the corner is Chapelle St Jean, an ancient hospice and pilgrimage centre. The temptation to be a permanent pilgrim in Montreuil is very great.

Option 9: Downriver to Angers

This full-day excursion visits the magnificent church of Cunault before cutting across country to the Château de Brissac and spending the day (or night) in historic Angers.

While the right bank of the Loire boasts the grand *levées* (banks) built by the Plantagenets, the south bank harbours more spiritual treasures. The wooded left bank is dotted with dolmens, Roman remains, ruined abbeys and, above all, delightful Romanesque churches at Chênehutte, Trèves, Cunault, Gennes, Bessé and St-Rémy-la-Varenne. This stretch of the Loire is also very good for nature-watching. Take a picnic and, while sitting near the sandbanks, look out for terns, cormorants, mallards and even ospreys.

Leave Saumur on the D751 and stop at **St Hilaire-St-Florent** for an early wine-tasting in **Veuve Amiot** (19 Rue Ackermann, 10–11.30am, 2.30–5.30pm). This area is second only to Champagne in the production of *méthode champenoise* wines. After watching the complex process of second fermentation, sample the best dry, floral-scented wines. Virtually next door is **Gratien et Meyer** (9–12am, 2–6pm), a celebrated grower of sparkling and fruity dessert wines.

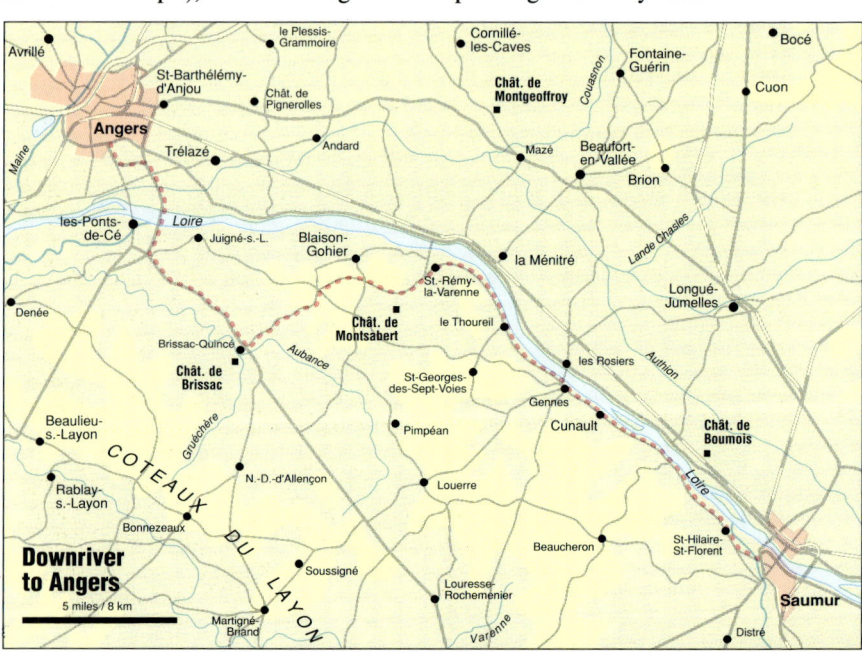

Typical Loire Valley countryside

From here, continue downriver to **Cunault**, one of the finest Romanesque churches in France. This priory church once answered to Tournus in Burgundy but its grandeur is now a counterpoint to the sleepy village. A squat 11th-century belltower dominates the north facade while the west side is adorned with a Madonna and Child. Inside, the height of the vaulted ceilings and the delicacy of the sculpted capitals create a sense of majesty. If you happen to be there at 11am on Sunday, attend Gregorian mass. Alternatively, consider returning for an organ recital at Cunault or chamber music at **Trèves**, a Romanesque church nearby.

Continue downriver along the D132 to **St-Rémy-la-Varenne**. En route, notice the churches and the Romanesque abbey of St-Maur. If you want a delicious fish lunch and a long afternoon in Angers, cross the river here and drive 4km (2½ miles) west to **La Bohalle**. Try the rustic **Auberge de la Gare** (Tel: 41 80 41 37). Consider staying nearby at **L'Hermitage** (Tel: 41 54 96 05), a charming guesthouse run by a Scot. The family may invite you to a traditional game of *boule de fort*, played with weighted balls. From here, take the fast D952 to Angers and follow signs to the **Château d'Angers**.

Alternatively, try the slow route to Angers, via Brissac-Quincé. From St-Rémy take the D55 through woods and vineyards to the **Château de Brissac** (9.30am–5.45pm). The château has been owned by the Ducs de Brissac for almost 500 years and is a hotch-potch of styles. The Duke calls it 'a half-

Angers Cathedral

16th-century carving

built new château built within a half-destroyed old castle'. The seven-storeyed building is flanked by medieval towers yet looks surprisingly elegant inside. The visit ends with a welcome *dégustation* of Anjou-Gamay wines.

From here take the D748 to **Angers**. The **Château** (9am–7pm, park beside the walls) looks forbidding, built out of dark schist by Blanche de Castille in 1228. Although the original castle was partially demolished during the Wars of Religion, the feudal atmosphere lingers in the ramparts, towers, moats and gardens. A gallery inside now houses *L'Apocalypse*, the finest tapestry series in the Loire. After the Revolution, these magnificent 14th-century tapestries were used as saddle-cloths and only rescued by a monk in 1848.

Afterwards, stroll through old Angers, bounded by the château and Rue du Mail. Walk down Rue St-Evroult to the Romanesque **Cathedral** and admire the sculpted facade and stained glass windows. On the adjoining **Place Ste Croix** notice a timber-framed house with carvings representing the tree of life. From here walk to bustling **Place du Ralliement** and sample honey-flavoured Côteaux du Layon wines or Cointreau, invented in Angers. Angers' most striking museum, **Galerie David d'Angers**, is at 33 Rue Toussaint (10am–1pm, 2–7pm).

The town's most prestigious restaurant is **Le Quéré** (3 Boulevard Foch, Tel: 41 20 00 20) but the whole town is a gastronomic delight. Consider a dinner cruise on **Le Roi René** (Quai de la Savatte, Tel: 41 88 37 47). **L'Entracte** (9 Louis-de-Romain, Tel: 41 87 71 82) is a gourmet regional restaurant, **Les Trois Rivières** (62 Promenade de Reculée, Tel: 41 73 31 88) a fish restaurant on the river. The best hotel-restaurant is **Anjou** (1 Boulevard Foch, Tel: 41 88 24 82) but for a comfortable hotel in the heart of town choose **Le Continental** (12 Rue Louis-de-Romain, Tel: 41 86 94 94). Angers is a lively cultural capital, particularly during the July Festival d'Anjou. For details, call the tourist office (Tel: 41 88 23 85).

The gardens at Château Angers

Staying In and Dining Out

$$$$ Luxury
$$$ Expensive
$$ Moderate
$ Inexpensive

Bourgueil

CHATEAU DES RÉAUX
Le Port-Boulet, 37140 Bourgueil.
Tel: 47 95 14 40
Gorgeous Renaissance château hotel. Dinner with charming owners. English spoken. (Port-Boulet exit off the N152). $$$

L'ECU DE FRANCE
14 Rue de Tours, 37140 Bourgueil.
Tel: 47 97 70 18.
Cosy hotel/restaurant. Seafood and regional dishes. $$

Fontevraud L'Abbaye

HOTELLERIE DU PRIEURÉ ST LAZARE
Abbaye Royale de Fontevraud,
49590 Fontevraud.
Tel: 41 51 73 16.
Hotel/restaurant within the abbey. Traditional or gourmet cuisine on terrace. Anjou/Touraine wines. Concerts. $$$

LE DOMAINE DE MESTRÉ
Mestré, 49590 Fontevraud.
Tel: 41 51 75 87 or 41 51 72 32.
Rooms in period country estate. Meals available. Signposted along D147, north of Fontevraud. English spoken. $$

LA LICORNE
Allée Ste Catherine, 49590 Fontevraud.
Tel: 41 51 72 49.
Restaurant with secluded courtyard near abbey. Lobster, oysters and asparagus, *chausson de chèvre chaud*. $$

Montreuil-Bellay

SPLENDID HOTEL
139 Rue Dr Gaudriez,
49260 Montreuil-Bellay.
Tel: 41 52 30 21 or 41 52 35 50.
Comfortable hotel with pool, garden. Regional restaurant. Request room in quiet, stylish annexe. $$

DEMEURE DES PETITS AUGUSTINS (B&B)
Place des Augustins,
49260 Montreuil-Bellay.
Tel: 41 52 33 88.
Elegant Renaissance mansion with courtyard in town centre. Quiet, comfortable, atmospheric rooms. $

Saumur

LE PRIEURÉ
49350 Chênehutte-les-Tuffeaux.
Tel: 41 67 90 14.
Hotel/restaurant in 15th-century priory overlooking the Loire. Pool. Angevin dishes. 6km (3¾ miles) west of Saumur. $$$$

HOTEL ANNE D'ANJOU
31 Quai Mayaud, 49400 Saumur.
Tel: 41 67 30 30.
Elegant 18th century town hotel with garden. Views of Loire and château. Gourmet restaurant. $$$

LES DÉLICES DU CHATEAU
Les Feuquières,
Château du Saumur, 49400 Saumur.
Tel: 41 67 65 60.
Gourmet restaurant overlooking the château. Book. $$$$

AUBERGE ST PIERRE
6 Place St Pierre,
Saumur, 49400 Saumur.
Tel: 41 51 26 25.
Regional restaurant: *coq au vin; rillettes maison*; pike in butter. Overlooks church and square. $$

Shopping

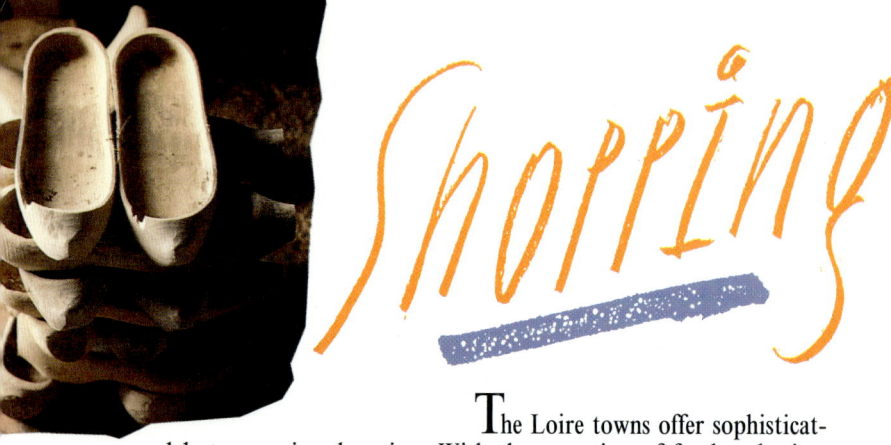

The Loire towns offer sophisticated but expensive shopping. With the exception of food and wine, this is not a region for bargains. However, for art-collectors, horse fanatics and even penniless browsers, the region is rewarding.

Shops generally open from 9am–12pm, 2–6.30pm but times are variable, particularly for *boulangeries* and *charcuteries*. Many shops close on Monday mornings while, in the cities, department stores often stay open at lunchtime. Markets are usually morning affairs. If planning a picnic lunch, buy the ingredients before setting out.

Antiques and Art

In **Tours**, Rue de la Scellerie is the place for antiques. There you can browse for old maps, paintings, Art Deco lamps and *ferronerie d'art* (wrought ironwork). In **Angers**, antique shops and galleries are centred on Rue Toussaint. L'Atelier (9 Rue Toussaint, Tel: 41 88 74 10) sells regional paintings while Galerie Toussaint (19bis Rue Toussaint, Tel: 41 88 38 58) specialises in modern art. For antiquarian books and prints, visit such *bouquinistes* as Gillard (13 Rue Toussaint, Tel: 41 88 66 15). Engraved slates are made by Christian Sauques (110 Rue Bressigny, Angers). In the smaller Loire towns, antiques tend to be imported and prices inflated.

Flea market, Beaufort-en-Vallée

Chinaware

Gien, along with Nevers, is noted for its distinctive chinaware so it is worth making the trip east of Orléans. Faienceries de Gien was founded by an Englishman in 1821 (Place de la Victoire, Gien, daily 9–12am, 2–6pm). Here you can look at rare pieces of *faience* or purchase seconds. For more chinaware, explore the shops around Place du Maréchal Leclerc. Plates can be decorated with Oriental, floral or royal motifs. The porcelain salamanders, porcupines and ermines are a reminder of the Loire's royal heyday.

Tours produces everyday china, *grès de Touraine*. These country-style designs are often hand-made and available in Petit St Martin, the lovely artisans' quarter of Tours. In the same area look out for curious-shaped receptacles for snails, *rillettes* and *pâtés*. This is also the place for pottery, candles, jewellery and a range of reasonably-priced crafts. For chinaware from Gien, Rouen or Touraine, visit Au Père Fragile in **Angers** (23 Rue St-Julien, Tel: 41 86 12 29).

Drinks
Fruit liqueurs and spirits make a change from Loire wines. In **Orléans** the speciality is a pear liqueur called La Poire d'Olivet, available from Covifruit (61 Rue du Pressoir-Tonneau; 9–12am, 2–6pm). In **Angers**, the obvious choice is Cointreau, invented in 1849 by a local boy. Visit L'Espace Cointreau, with its museum, distillery and bar (Carrefour Molière, St-Barthélemy, Tel: 41 43 25 21).

Food
The Loire is well-provided with *vente directe* outlets. En route, look out for signs advertising *dégustations* (wine), *fromage de chèvre* (goat's cheese), *miel* (honey) and other treats. Hand-made chocolates are excellent, particularly in Angers, Tours and Saumur. In Angers, try La Petite Marquise (22 Rue des Lices, Tel: 41 87 43 01). In Tours, pralines and stuffed prunes are on sale at La Chocolatière (4 Rue de la Scellerie, Tel: 47 05 66 75). Many delicacies are easily transported: *pruneaux farcis* (stuffed prunes), Sologne honey and Orléans *cotignac* (quince jelly) make unusual presents.

Leather
Leather goods are a sound buy in **Orléans** and the **Sologne**. These include leather jackets, belts, boots and riding gear. La Sellerie (17 Rue des Lices, Angers, Tel: 41 88 07 56) produces pricey horsey goods. Hunting, shooting and fishing equipment is Sologne's speciality. Animal-lovers may wish to steer clear of the trinkets made from local wildlife. Shoe shops abound in Tours and Orléans.

Markets
Every town has a weekly morning market and cities like Angers and Tours have daily markets. Check times locally. **Angers**' biggest flea market covers the town centre on Saturday mornings. **Tours** has a popular flower market on Boulevard Béranger on Wednesday and Saturday mornings. Wickerwork is available in markets but best at **Villaines-les-Rochers** (see Option 5).

Antique dealer in Vatan

Eating

The Loire marches on its stomach. Game and mushrooms from the forests, asparagus from the Sologne, fish from the Loire. Food is both robust and refined. Moving down the Loire from east to west traces a varied gastronomic feast from creamy pike in the Orléanais region to venison in the Sologne, *charcuterie* in Touraine and veal in Anjou. Few can resist tasting the quality of life in the Garden of France.

Orléanais
The region around Orléans is a good starter to the Loire feast. *Andouillettes de Jargeau* are reputedly the best of France's succulent sausages. *Pigeon à la crapaudine* is a boned and broiled pigeon. *Brochet à l'Orléanais* is pike cooked in a shallot and egg sauce. Orléans also boasts several pungent goats' cheeses. Honey, strawberries and cherries star in desserts and sweet liqueurs. *Noisette*, made from hazelnuts, is the most aromatic of local liqueurs.

Blésois
Blésois, the region based on Blois, lives off the Sologne woods and the cereal-growing plains. Blois produces tasty game terrine but fish is not neglected. Trout, carp or pike *à la Chambord* means a lavish dish stuffed with fish *purée* and truffles from the woods. However, arrival in Blois is sweetened by the overpowering aroma of chocolate from the *Poulain* chocolate factory. It also confirms the city's sweet tooth, a tradition going back to the days when cocoa was shipped here from the East Indies via Nantes.

Sologne
The marshy and wooded area south of Blois grows strawberries, asparagus and spring vegetables. But it is even better-known as a game-lover's paradise. Every autumn, rustic restaurants are full of feathered and furry game. *Marcassin* (wild boar), venison and

pheasant appear on menus with other forest delicacies such as *cèpes* (boletus) and *girolles* (chanterelle) mushrooms.

Touraine
Touraine produces *charcuterie* delicacies such as *rillettes* and *rillons*. *Rillettes* are creamy *pâtés* made from minced duck, goose or pork and served chilled in earthenware pots. *Rillons*, chunky pork morsels, are served cold as rustic *hors d'oeuvres*. *Quiche Tourangelle* is a flan weighed down by liberal dollops of *rillons* and *rillettes*. Equally substantial are *crêpes Tourangelles*, buckwheat pancakes stuffed with spinach, ham, cheeses or fruit. Tours' melons, pears and plums have been prized since Renaissance times and find their way into desserts or fruit liqueurs like *eau de vie poires William* and *eau de vie de pruneaux*.

Anjou
Anjou prides itself on *andouillettes*. These spicy tripe sausages are produced all over France but are particularly tasty in Angers and Tours. *Cul-de-veau à la angevine* is rump of veal in a rich sauce of white wine and brandy. *Alose de Loire farcie à l'angevine* is shad stuffed with eggs and shallots before being drenched in a bottle of dry white *vin d'Anjou*. Angers is also known for its fruit liqueurs and apple desserts. These combine in *crêpes angevines*, filled with

Loire delicacies

apples and drenched in Cointreau, the local liqueur. *Soufflé au Cointreau* is a lighter variant on the theme.

Fish

Many delicacies have crossed their original borders and fish dishes in particular are rarely restricted to one region. Salmon, pike, shad, grey mullet, carp, trout, pike-perch are all fished in the Sologne's lakes or in the Loire and its tributaries. *Petite friture de la Loire* is staple fare, delicious in La Daguenière and La Bohalle, villages east of Angers. Other fish delicacies are *brème farcie* (stuffed bream) and *quenelles* (pike dumplings). *Sandre* (pike-perch) often replaces salmon and pike on the menu. Fish is usually served simply with a *beurre blanc* sauce. *Alose* (shad) is served with *beurre blanc* on a bed of sorrel cooked in cream. *Matelote d'anguilles*, eel stewed in red wine with mushrooms, onions and prunes, is common in Anjou and Touraine. (In the less traditional recipe, tomatoes and bacon replace prunes.)

Meat

Meat dishes, whether *hors d'oeuvres* or main courses, tend to be filling. As starters, there are rich *pâtés* and terrines from goose or duck liver. (*Foie gras* farms can be visited in the Sologne.) The adventurous might like *biquet en pot*, goat *pâté*, only available in April and June. Roast goat is usually served in a raspberry sauce. In rustic restaurants, *boudin blanc* (chicken sausage) or *boudin noir*, grilled black pudding, are washed down with *rosé* wine. To follow, there may be *compote de lapereau*, rabbit stew cooked in Vouvray wine. *Noisette de porc aux pruneaux*, pork tenderloin with prunes, was originally from Touraine. If the thought of prunes is off-putting, bear in mind that prunes soaked in a bottle of Vouvray are unrecognisable.

Chicken is a safe choice, whether served as a *fricassée de volaille* in mushroom sauce or as *coq au vin*. This casserole can be cooked in red Chinon, mellow Bourgueil or sweet white Vouvray. Drink the same wine with the meal. If you are thinking of making *coq au vin* at home, remember that the *vin* element means at least a bottle. Wine aside, there is little consolation for vegetarians. A request for an *assiette de crudités* can be rewarding but chefs prefer to serve a single select vegetable to a profusion of the best in season. Even so, asparagus, wild mushrooms and Saumur's *champignons de Paris* are some compensation, as are goats' cheeses.

Speciality sausages

Goat's cheeses

Cheese

The Loire is not a great area for cheeses but the goats' cheeses are excellent, particularly *Sainte-Maure*, *Valençay* and *crottin de Chavignol*. The latter comes from Berry, the southern Loire region, and is served warm on a bed of walnuts and lettuce. Salads are often dressed with walnut oil.

Orléans boasts *cendré d'Olivet*, a round cheese matured in wood ash and served in walnut leaves. *Crémet d'Angers* is a creamy dessert cheese rather like ricotta. It is often eaten with strawberries. The cheeses are best bought in markets or direct from makers (labels marked *fermier* are a guarantee of fresh farm produce). Unfortunately, European Community regulations may ultimately shorten the lives of these and other French artisanal and regional cheeses.

Dessert

Desserts include apricot tart, Corméry macaroons and sweet *pâtisseries* from Tours. *Amandin aux belles angevines* is a sweet made from pears, almonds and liqueur. But the most celebrated dessert is *Tarte Tatin*, an upside-down apple tart. This rich caramelised dish was supposedly invented in the last century by the Tatin sisters from Sologne.

According to Curnonsky, the great chef from Angers, "True Tourangelle cuisine takes its inspiration from the wit of Rabelais and the genius of Descartes . . . it is clear, logical and straightforward". Judge for yourself. *Bon appétit*.

Eating Out

Wine

'Shooting stars in September, barrels overflowing in November' says a local proverb. If so, there must have been a sky of shooting stars recently. Loire wines have improved dramatically in the 1990s, winning major wine competitions. Specific growers are mentioned in this book's Itineraries but tourist offices also have lists of wine fairs and *vignerons*. Choose wines from a single grower, rather than blended wines. Angers, Saumur and Tours have showrooms for Loire wines. (Contact Maison du Vin de l'Anjou, 5 bis Place Kennedy, 49000 Angers.)

The main grape varieties are Cabernet Franc, Chenin Blanc, Sauvignon Blanc, Gamay and Pinot Noir. Cabernet Franc is responsible for the blackcurrant-scented reds while Gamay produces gentle, Beaujolais-type reds. Pinot Noir creates aromatic reds and *rosés*. Sauvignon Blanc is refreshing and tangy and, at best, produces wines like Sancerre. Chenin Blanc is a late-ripening white grape which, in a poor season, produces harsh whites but in a great one can make mature sweet wines. The following are a selection of the most *gouleyant* (tasty). As Balzac said, "Shame on those who don't love Touraine's valleys flowing with wine".

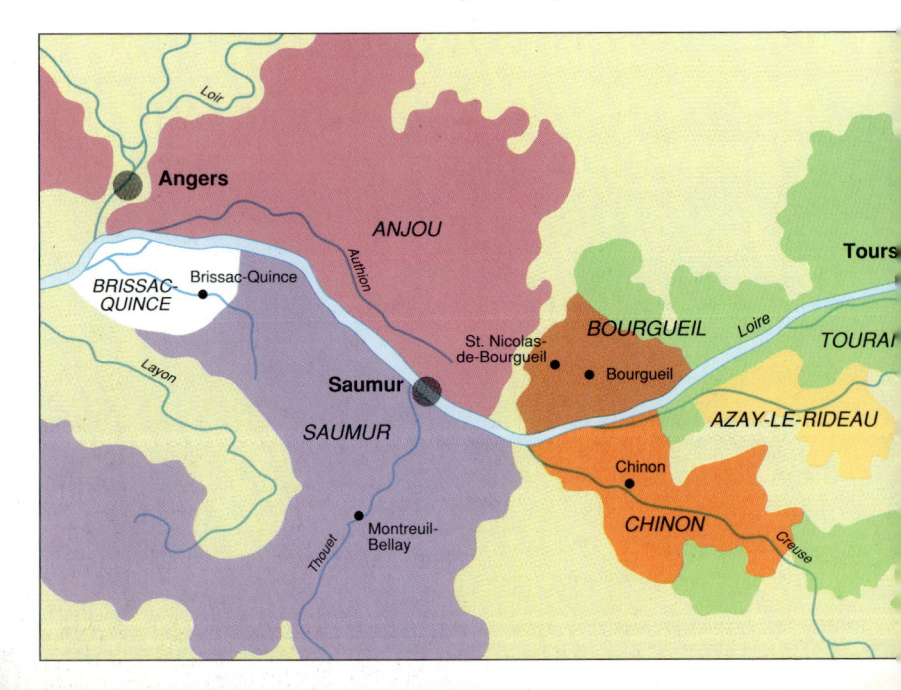

Anjou Rosé
Like Muscadet, this was once a poor-quality wine bar staple but has improved. Ideally, it should be fresh, pink and taste of apple and nuts. Try *rosé* from Brissac with *crudités* or *charcuteries*. Cabernet d'Anjou is a superior *rosé*.

Bourgueil & St Nicolas-de-Bourgueil
Made from the Cabernet Franc grape, these earthy wines go well with meat, game or *matelote d'anguilles* (See Dining). Bourgueil, like Chinon and Vouvray, matures beautifully.

Cheverny
Cheverny is known for its aromatic dry wines. The white wine makes a good *apéritif*; the *rosé* goes well with cold meats. As for the fruity red wines, try Christian Tessier's award-winning Cheverny Rouge, made from the Pinot Noir grape.

Chinon
Chinon, made from the Cabernet Franc grape, was the full-bodied red wine beloved by Rabelais. Drunk young or mature, it accompanies chicken, red meat, game and cheeses.

Coteaux du Layon
Grown on the prairies south of Angers, the whites are made from the Chenin Blanc and can be dry or sweet. If tasted at Domaine des Hauts-Perrays (Chaudefonds-sur-Layon, Tel: 41 78 04 38), there is a free *dégustation* of regional foods too.

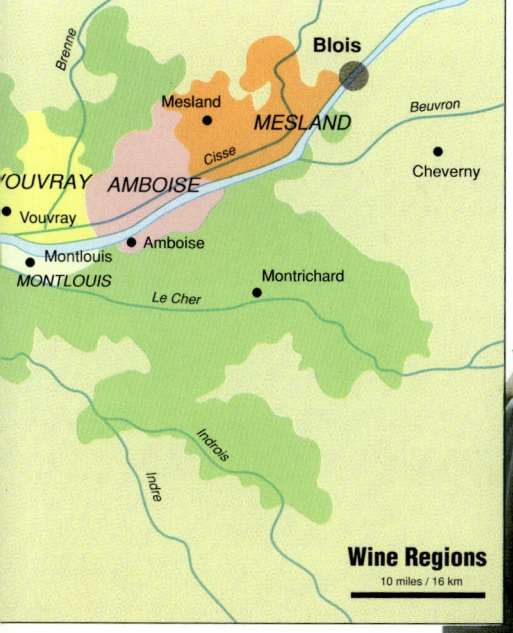

Wine Regions
10 miles / 16 km

Muscadet
Muscadet, just outside the region covered by this guide, this was the bland drink of 1980s wine bars. Discriminating drinkers now choose Muscadet sur Sèvre et Maine sur Lie, with its honeyed yet peppery note ideal for oysters and fish.

Saumur
Saumur is a diverse wine-growing region, producing a fruity red Saumur Champigny and a dry *rosé*, Cabernet de Saumur. But Saumur is best known for its sparkling wines produced by the Champagne method. Brut produced by Ackerman, Gratien & Meyer or Veuve Amiot rivals Champagne in quality and makes an extremely refreshing *apéritif*.

Touraine
Made from the Sauvignon Blanc grape, a good Touraine rivals a Sancerre. These fruity yet dry white wines are refreshing rather than memorable but are excellent with Loire fish. Touraine reds, made from the Gamay grape, lack the power of a Bourgueil or Chinon but go well with local meat dishes.

Vouvray & Montlouis
These rivals face one another across the Loire but Vouvray overshadows Montlouis. Made from Chenin Blanc, these whites can be bone dry, *demi-sec* or sweet, still or sparkling. Trout is excellent poached in Vouvray – and drunk with Vouvray wine. Sweet Vouvray is the ideal dessert wine.

Vineyard from the air

Nightlife

The Loire is not the place for chic nightclubs and shows, although Tours and Angers are the trendiest cities. As befits the most civilised region in France, there is a wide range of cultural entertainment on offer, with emphasis on music, ballet and drama. In summer, there are classical concerts in châteaux and converted barns, troglodyte caves and Romanesque churches. For most visitors, however, the ideal evening entertainment is *son et lumière*.

Son et Lumière

These increasingly sophisticated shows are a romantic way of appreciating architecture while indulging in time travel. Performances are held at about 10pm on summer evenings. Entrance fees are relatively high (30–100 francs) but are good value for special occasions. The shows can either be classic sound and light shows (as at Blois) or pageants acted and danced by large casts (as at Le Lude). Several shows have an English version but even if the performance is in French, there is usually enough spectacle to compensate for linguistic misunderstandings. The current trend is towards costume drama, fireworks and audience participation. Check dates and times with local tourist offices.

Amboise: brash and jaunty account of the château in the time of François I. Horses, lavish costumes and fireworks.

Azay-le-Rideau: amateurish but romantic. We accompany the actors around a moat dotted with Renaissance boats.

Beaugency: costume drama held on the banks of the Loire.

Blois: compelling history with Renaissance facade as star (English version).

Chambord: grand new historical spectacle with huge cast. Horses, dancing, lasers, fireworks. (English version).

Son et lumière pageant

Chédigny: changing theme. Held in a small village south of Tours. All the village participates. (Tel: 47 92 51 43).
Chenonceau: emphasises the romantic past and female tradition.
Cheverny: hunting theme. Fireworks, fountains, lasers.
Le Lude: the most prestigious show. A sweep of five centuries of French history acted and danced by villagers.
Loches: Joan of Arc theme in the château she visited.
Saché: Balzac's life. Actors; fireworks.

Bars and Nightclubs

As university towns, Angers and Tours are the liveliest centres, with piano bars, cocktail bars, jazz clubs, nightclubs, beer halls and café-théâtres. **Angers:** Number One, 5 bis Avenue Vauban (Tel: 41 87 31 41) is a huge disco with two dance floors. Le Toulouse (35 Rue de la Roe, Tel: 41 86 16 16) is a typical, relaxed piano bar while Le Topaze (Bar Péniche, Tel: 41 88 30 01) is a jazz café. **Tours:** bars are in and around Rue de la Rôtisserie. The best café-théâtres are le Bâteau Ivre (rock bands) and le Petit Faucheux (balladeers, jazz bands and poets). (For information, Tel: 47 05 58 08.)

Live Arts

Angers: As France's centre for contemporary dance and drama, Angers boasts the Centre National du Danse Contemporaine and Théâtre d'Angers as well as a major orchestra. (Book at the tourist office, Tel: 41 88 69 93.) **Blois:** summer church concerts and a range of live events in La Halle aux Grains (Place de la République, Tel: 54 74 21 22). **Fontevraud:** the ancient abbey holds exhibitions and concerts (Tel: 41 51 73 52). **Tours:** major classical singers and conductors perform summer concerts in a fabulous tithe barn, La Grange de Meslay (Parçay-Meslay, Tel: 47 29 19 29). Le Grand Théâtre stages classical drama while l'Autruche Théâtre opts for contemporary plays. (Contact the tourist office, Tel: 47 05 58 08).

Amboise at night

Calendar of Special Events

The Loire festival season is largely a summer show and consists of concerts, markets, pageants and *son et lumière* displays. Autumn is the time for harvest festivals, with most villages holding an apple, chestnut, wine or plum fair. Out of season, the Loire concentrates on trade fairs and its lively arts scene. Dates may change slightly so do check locally. Angers, Blois, Tours and Orléans tourist offices produce listings of regional events.

Journées d'Animations En Milieu Rural (June to October, Tel: 41 67 13 12) are organised days out which visit anything from an angora, game or silk farm to a clog-maker or cheese-maker. The day out involves food, drink and chat with the farmers so reasonable French is at least helpful. For details of this and all other events contact the relevant tourist office.

JANUARY–APRIL

Foire aux Vins (January, Angers): wine fair and competition.
Festival de Théâtre Masqué (March, Angers): masked drama.
Dimanches Animés de Cunault (April–September): craft market.
Foire de Pâques (Bourgueil): Easter fair near Saumur.

MAY

Festival de Chambord (also June): theatre, music and dance.
Fêtes de Jeanne d'Arc (7–9th, Orléans): Joan of Arc pageant.
Foire aux Vins (Vouvray): wine fair near Tours.
Gala du Cadre Noir (Saumur): international horse show.

JUNE

Foire aux Fromages (1st–3rd, Ste Maure): cheese fair.
Fête de la Musique (Chinon): classical concerts.
Fêtes Musicales (Grange de Meslay); fortnight of classical concerts and

recitals in magnificent tithe barn near Tours.
Game Fair (Chambord): sampling of game and fish.
Tuffolies (June–September, Saumur): military music, flower shows and historical pageants (events vary each year).
Sully International Festival (mid-June to mid-July): chamber music and recitals in churches and châteaux near Orléans.
Journées d'Animations Rurales (until October): see above.

JULY

Angers l'Eté (Angers): dance, circus, theatre, music.
Classical concerts (Tours): in gardens and châteaux nearby.
Festival d'Anjou (all over Anjou): concerts, plays.
Festival Estival (also August, Amboise): concerts.
Festival de Jazz d'Orléans (Orléans): jazz stars.
Festival Chorégraphique (Tours): modern dance festival.
Foire aux Boudins (20th, Chenonceaux): black pudding fair.
Foire des Vignerons (21st, Bourgueil): red wine fair.
Foire à l'Ail (26th, Tours): garlic and basil market.
Heures Musicales (Cunault, Trèves): church concerts.
Journées de la Rose (Doué-la-Fontaine): rose displays.
Musi-Troglo (Saumur): concerts in troglodyte caves.
Musique, Vins et Sites (Anjou): scenic concerts with wine.
Théâtre Musical (Loches): outdoor concerts near the château.
14 Juillet: Bastille day; fireworks and street parties everywhere.

AUGUST

Marché Médiéval (1st weekend, Chinon): medieval market.
Foire aux Vins (15th, Amboise and Vouvray): wine fairs.
Fête des Vins de Loire (15th, Bourgueil): wine festival.
Marché à l'Ancienne (3rd weekend, Chinon): period market.
Foire aux Melons (25th, Saché): melon fair south of Tours.

SEPTEMBER

Art et Lumière (Fontevraud): concerts in the ancient abbey.
Festival de Folklore (Angers): international folk festival.
Festival de Jazz (Montlouis): jazz festival near Tours.
Foire aux Vins (15th, Tours): wine fair in old quarter.
Foire aux Vins (Beaugency): wine fair by the river.
Foire de Septembre (10th, Bourgueil): wine and food feast.
Horse and Hunt Fair (La Ferté-St-Aubin, Tel: 38 76 52 72).

OCTOBER

Journées Gastronomiques (Romorantin): food and game fair.
Foire aux Pommes (26th, Azay-le-Rideau): apple fair.
Foire aux Chèvres (27th, Céré-la-Ronde): goat market.
Apple, chestnut, game, plum festivals in most villages.

NOVEMBER/DECEMBER

Concours des Rouges de Brissac (November, Château de Brissac): red wine competition south of Angers.

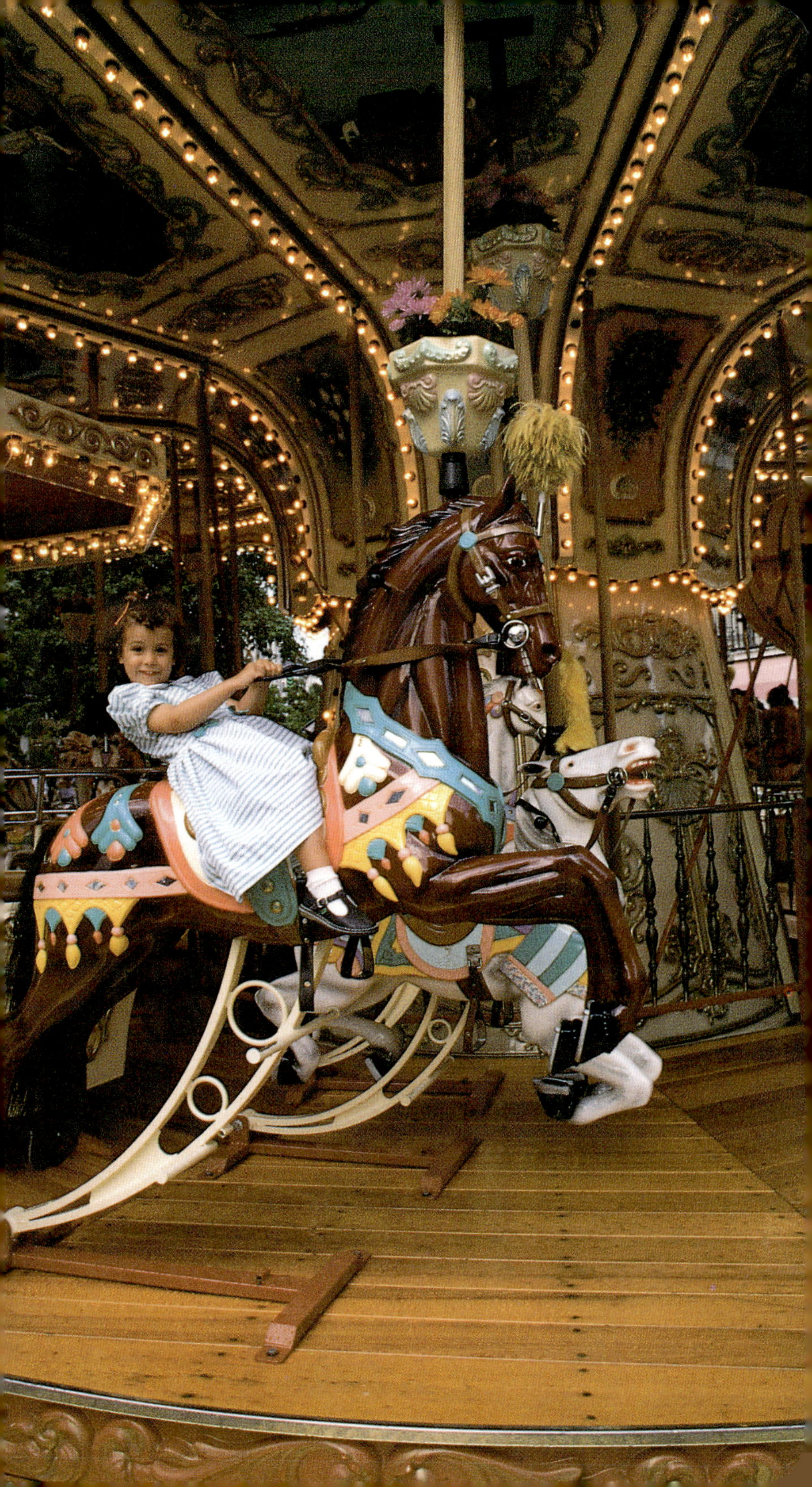

Practical Information

TRAVEL ESSENTIALS

When to Visit
For sunshine, balmy evenings and a wide range of cultural events, visit in the summer. The peak season is July and August, when the *son et lumière* programme is in full swing. The only snag is that roads on the châteaux circuit can be crowded and accommodation needs to be booked well in advance. Late spring and early autumn are the loveliest seasons as far as the landscape is concerned.

June is warm, uncrowded and yet culturally lively while September is an excellent time for wine and food festivals. However, bear in mind that outside the summer months the weather is unpredictable and the châteaux have slightly restricted visiting times. Average temperatures are: May 22°C (71F); August 26°C (78F); and September 20°C (68F).

GETTING THERE

By Air
Air France operates an infrequent service between London Gatwick and Saint-Symphorien, near Tours (UK Tel: 071-499 9511). No flights connect Paris and the Loire Valley. Passengers who arrive at a Paris airport will therefore need to drive or take the fast TGV train to the Loire.

By Sea
From the UK, Brittany Ferries run services from Portsmouth to Caen and St Malo, convenient ports for the Loire (Tel: 0705-827701). The ships are well-equipped and the staff friendly. Invest in a cabin. Alternatively travel by the comfortable P&O European Ferries from Portsmouth to Le Havre (Tel: 0705-827677).

By Train
A convenient option from Paris, particularly since the fast TGV service reaches Vendôme in 42 minutes, Tours in 57 minutes and Angers in 90 minutes. Car hire is available from main stations. Contact SNCF in London (Tel: 071-499 2153) or Paris (Tel: 1-45 08 41) for information in English.

By Road
From Paris the fast A10 leads to the Loire, with Orléans just over an hour's drive, Blois reached in 1 hour 40 minutes and Tours in just over 2 hours. From St Malo, Angers is 200km (124 miles) away. From Caen, Orléans is about 240km (149 miles).

GETTING AROUND

By Train
Travelling by train will not allow you to follow the Itineraries in this guide. The Loire is best visited by car. However, certain châteaux are close to stations. (Ask the SNCF for their leaflet *Les Châteaux de la Loire en Train*). Consider getting a *France Vacances* Pass.

By Coach
The major towns run guided summer day trips to the major châteaux and to evening *son et lumière*. The standard of guiding (in English) is quite high but one inevitably feels 'packaged'. However, if you are based in Tours or Angers and don't feel like driving all the time, these tours are a sensible option. With the exception of Blois, public transport outside the main towns is not very good.

By Shuttle
Blois runs an excellent shuttle service to the main sights in the region (including Amboise, Chambord and Cheverny). Called *La Navette des Châteaux*, the service runs from mid-June to early September and includes a 'passport' with discounts on châteaux entrances. Book trips at the TLC (Transports Loir-et-Cher) booth at Blois station (Tel: 54 78 15 66). To avoid daily driving, Blois is the best base.

By Car
The only way to explore all the Itineraries in this guide. Car hire is expensive but easily organised at main stations. Comprehensive insurance is recommended. Speed limits are 130kph (80mph) on motorways, 110 kph (68mph) on dual carriageways, 90kph (56mph) on other roads and 60kph (37mph) in towns. I'd advise travellers to get the good Institut Géographique National (IGN) Val de

New use for old buildings

Loire map (Red Series, 1cm: 2.5km).

Priorité à la droite is now less difficult for foreign drivers. All major roads have right of way (marked *passage protégé*). You must give way to traffic already on a roundabout. *Priorité* does still apply in built-up areas where no priority is marked. (This means that you must give way to motorists coming from a side turning to the right.)

Road Signs: look out for signs saying *cedez le passage* and *vous n'avez pas la priorité* which require you to give way. Other key signs are: *chaussée déformée* (poor road surface); *déviation* (diversion); *péage* (toll); *ralentir* (slow down); *sauf riverains* (entry prohibited except to residents); *sens unique* (one-way street); *serrez à droite/gauche* (keep right/left); *stationnement interdit* (no parking); *toutes directions* (all routes). **Garage French:** I've had a breakdown (*Ma voiture est en panne*); *l'essence* (petrol); *l'huile* (oil); *le plein, s'il vous plaît* (full tank, please); *sans plomb/normal/super* (lead-free/normal/super).

ACCOMMODATION

The Loire probably has the widest range of accommodation in France, offering everything from exclusive châteaux-hotels and prestigious city hotels to rustic *auberges* (inns) and friendly *chambres d'hôtes* (Bed and Breakfast). I have selected the best from different style and price categories.

Hotels

If you wish to select your own accommodation, the tourist office's official *Centre Val de Loire Hotel Guide* is a useful listing (in English and French). In summer, you may be expected to accept half-board so enquire beforehand. The following loose hotel groupings operate in the Loire.

Châteaux Accueil: châteaux which accept paying guests.

Relais et Châteaux: luxurious four-star hotels.

Relais du Silence: 2–4 star hotels in tranquil settings.

Logis de France: the yellow and green castle sign denotes a small 1 or 2-star hotel, often a family-run inn.

Gîtes de France: rural farms or cottages, usually let by the week. (Lists available from regional tourist offices.)

Chambres d'Hôtes: these are a wonderful way of exploring the Loire. They are graded according to a star system (from ✯ for basic to ✯✯✯✯ for special) according to site, comfort and character. The ones recommended in this guide are all ✯✯ or above. They are equal or superior to a ✯✯ hotel. Obtain a list from tourist offices or buy the complete country guide, *French Country Welcome*. One important consideration is that these B&B are situated in small towns and villages. Some are very rural so a good map is essential. In summer, book (by phone) at least a couple of days in advance. If you want the *repas d'hôte* (dinner *en famille*), you need to speak good French or check whether your hosts speak English. For accommodation only, basic French is helpful but inessential.

Classification

At the end of each of the five regional sections you will find a hotel/restaurant listing. The $ symbols used refer to the price categories below and do not necessarily coincide with tourist board listings.

Accommodation: French hotels usually charge by the room, rather than the person, so the following price categories refer to a double room. In $$$ and $$$$ hotels there may be an additional charge for breakfast, especially for a full 'American' breakfast. $ = up to 250FF, $$ = 250-400FF, $$$ = 400-700FF, $$$$ = 700-1,500FF.

Restaurants: dining recommendations are listed according to the rough price categories below. Remember, however, that the set menu (*le menu à prix fixe*) is always much cheaper than dining *à la carte*. Also note that even inexpensive restaurants ($$) can offer a second *menu gastronomique* at a much higher price. This is the rough cost of dinner for one, with local wine: $ = under 100FF, $$ = 100-150FF, $$$ = 200-300FF, $$$$ = 300-500FF.

BUSINESS HOURS

Banks
Open 8.30am–12pm, 2–4.30pm weekdays. In big cities they are often open on Saturday morning but closed on Monday. Take your passport when cashing travellers' cheques or Eurocheques. Credit cards are widely accepted in higher grade hotels and restaurants. Cash dispensers outside Paris may not able to process foreign credit cards and Eurocheque cards.

Châteaux and Museums
This book gives summer châteaux times. The major châteaux are open 9am–6/7pm daily. But hours are restricted out of season and many close for a couple of hours at lunch. For a comprehensive listing of opening times get the *Châteaux Country* brochure from any tourist office. While châteaux are usually open every day, museums tend to close on Monday or Tuesday.

MEDIA & COMMUNICATION

Daily Press
Ouest France and *La Nouvelle République du Centre Ouest* have large circulations and are often read in preference to national dailies. Excellent monthly magazines cover customs, architecture and events: *Le Magazine de Touraine*; *Le Journal de Sologne* and *Le Magazine du Berry*.

Telephone
Many public telephone boxes now accept phonecards (*télécartes*), which can be bought from Post Offices and *tabacs*.

To dial other countries first dial the international access code 19, wait for the second bleep, then the country code: Australia (61); Germany (49); Italy (39); Japan (81); Netherlands (31); Spain (34); UK (44); US and Canada (1). If you are using a US credit phone card, dial the company's access number below – Sprint, Tel: 19 0087; AT&T, Tel: 19 0011; MCI, Tel: 19 00 19.

ACTIVITIES

Ballooning
Buddy Bombard Balloon Adventures (June to October, Tel: 80 26 63 30). Called 'aerial nature walks', these trips float over the main châteaux,

dropping low enough to let you pick leaves or chat to passers-by. Similar trips can be booked at Angers tourist office (Tel: 41 88 69 93).

Boating
Anjou boasts the greatest number of navigable rivers in France, with **L'Oudon, Maine, Mayenne** and **Sarthe**. Cruises start near Angers. For short or long cruises, call Anjou Plaisance (Tel: 41 95 68 95) or Sarthe Fluviale (Tel: 41 73 14 16). For dinner cruises try Anjou Croisières (Tel: 41 88 37 47). **La Loire:** short boat trips from Chaumont (Tel: 54 20 70 70). **Le Loir:** 60km (37¼ miles) should be open for boating from late 1992 (Tel: 54 77 05 07). **Le Thouet:** kayaks hired in Montreuil-Bellay (Tel: 41 52 32 39). Water sports are popular on lakes near Angers and Tours. Angers' Lac de Maine leisure park is well-organised (Tel: 47 48 57 01).

Boule de Fort
A traditional game played all over Anjou. This variant on *boules* is played with weighted balls on a concave floor. The aim is to land by the *maître*, the tiny ball. Games are run by local associations and end in hearty drinking sessions. To play, contact Angers' regional tourist office (Tel: 41 88 23 85).

Cycling
Bicycles can be hired from main stations (Amboise, Blois, Tours etc). Other hire firms are: Sports Motos Cycles, 6 Rue Henri-Drussy, Blois (Tel: 54 78 02 64); and M Cosnet, Place de la République, Cour-Cheverny (Tel: 54 79 93 21).

Fishing
Salmon, eel and pike are fished in the Loire. For fishing in Anjou, contact Fédération de Pêche du Maine-et-Loire (14 Allée du Haras, 49100 Angers, Tel: 41 87 57 09). Blois regional tourist office organises salmon fishing trips in spring (Tel: 54 78 55 50).

Golf
The Loire now boasts 35 courses. In Anjou try Golf Club d'Angers (St Jean des Mauvrets, Tel: 41 91 96 56). For a new 18-hole course try Golf du Château, Cheverny (Tel: 54 79 24 70). Blois regional tourist office organises golfing holidays (Tel: 54 78 62 52).

Helicopter Flights
For parachute drops and flights in Anjou, contact Aéroclub de Saumur (Tel: 41 50 20 27). For helicopter flights over Touraine, contact Touraine Hélicoptère (Tel 47 24 81 44). For flights over Chambord and Cheverny, contact Blois tourist office (Tel: 54 74 06 49).

Riding

Anjou is France's riding centre. Hire horses near Angers from Eperon d'Angers, Route de Nantes, Beaucouzé (Tel: 41 48 23 25). Explore the Sologne on horseback with Les Ecuries de la Boulardière, Vernou-en-Sologne (Tel: 54 98 21 33). Or see Sologne by carriage (Tel: 54 78 55 50). Consider travelling in a horse-drawn caravan (*en roulotte*) between Chinon and Rabelais' house (Tel: 47 95 97 87). To watch equestrian displays or tour the prestigious Cadre Noir stables, visit Saumur (Tel: 41 51 03 06).

Rural Visits

Trips to local farms and craftspeople make a change from châteaux and provide insights into rural life. In the Sologne, for instance, you can visit a cabinet-maker, a potter, a goat farmer or a dried flower designer. (Get the *Sologne à Tout Coeur* list of addresses from Cour-Cheverny tourist office, Tel: 54 79 95 63). Alternatively consider a day trip organised by local tourist offices. (See *Journées d'Animation en Milieu Rural*, in the *Calendar of Special Events* section).

Walking

Blois, Orléans, Saumur and Tours tourist offices organise excellent thematic walking tours around town. The Loire is excellent hiking country with thousands of marked paths. For a gentle country ramble, the loveliest stretch is Balzac's route, between Azay-le-Rideau and Artannes (See Option 5). For serious hiking, follow the Grande Randonnée No 3 path through the Loire. Contact Blois or Tours regional tourist offices for routes. Also get the detailed IGN maps and the Loire Valley *Topoguides*, ramblers' guides with advice on routes and accommodation. A useful book is *Walks in the Loire Valley*, published by Robertson-McCarta in the *Footpaths of Europe* series.

Wildlife Watching

The watery Sologne is the obvious place so contact Romorantin tourist office (Tel: 54 76 43 89).
Animals: Chambord's vast grounds contain many observation posts *(aires de vision)*. To spot deer and wild boar, the best times are sunrise and sunset. Beaver-spotting trips can be organised by Beaugency tourist office. Blois regional tourist office organises trips to watch wildlife at night or to paint plants and birds in the Sologne (Tel: 54 78 55 50).
Birds: It is said that the Loire is Europe's last wild river and its shifting sands provide great bird-watching opportunities. Kingfishers, herons, terns, wild ducks and golden plover are just a few of the 290 species visible. Try the left bank at Parnay or further downriver, between Cunault and St-Rémy. In Sologne visit lakes such as Etang de Bézard.

CHILDREN

The Loire is not the most obvious choice for young children: traipsing round châteaux is not their idea of fun. However, the following suggestions should help.
Nature Trips: Blois regional tourist office organises excursions, including beaver-spotting on the Loire and watching wildlife at night (Tel: 54 78 55 50).
Aquariums: Loire fish in Montreuil-Bellay (Tel: 41 52 32 39); tropical fish in the Château de Tours (Tel: 47 64 29 52).
Châteaux: children always enjoy Chambord (horse dis-

plays at 11.45 and 5pm); Chaumont (wild grounds); Chenonceau (train ride, boat trips, nursery); Cheverny (try to be there in time for the feeding of the hounds at 5pm).

Cycling: bikes (both mountain and road versions) can be hired by the hour for safe rides around the grounds of Chambord (Tel: 54 20 34 86).

Museums: Leonardo da Vinci models in Clos Lucé (Tel: 47 57 00 73); animated wine museum at Chinon (Tel: 47 93 25 63).

Son et Lumière: choose a dramatic one with acting, dancing and fireworks. Chambord recommended (English version).

Swimming: unfortunately this is only allowed in the rivers Cher, Indre and Thouet (forbidden in the Loire because of quicksands and currents). Most river-side towns have a *plage*, a beach set aside for swimming.

Troglodytes: for visits to underground farms, caverns and restaurants see previous itineraries Day 5 and Option 7.

Waxworks: the Sleeping Beauty models in the Château d'Ussé; the historical Musée Grevin in Tours (Tel: 47 61 02 95).

Zoo: well-presented troglodyte zoo in an old quarry (Doué-la-Fontaine, Tel: 41 59 18 58). Snow leopards, monkeys etc.

USEFUL INFORMATION

Consulates
The nearest British Consulate is at 6 Rue La Fayette, 44000 Nantes (Tel: 40 48 57 47). In Paris the British Consulate is at 16 Rue d'Anjou, 75008 Paris (Tel: 1-42 66 91 42). The Irish Embassy is at 12 Avenue Foch, 75116 Paris (Tel: 1-45 00 20 87). The American Embassy is at 2 Avenue Gabriel, 75382 Paris, Cedex 08 (Tel: 1-42 96 12 02).

French Tourist Offices Abroad
Great Britain: Maison de la France, 178 Piccadilly, London W1V 0AL (Tel: 071-491 7622).
Ireland: 35 Lower Abbey St, Dublin 1, Eire (Tel: 771871).
United States: Maison de la France, 610 Fifth Avenue, New York, NY 10020-2452 (Tel: 212-757 1125).

Loire Tourist Offices
These are an invaluable source of information and help. Known as Syndicats d'Initiative or Offices du Tourisme, they are found in all towns. In villages the Mairie (Town Hall) may double as the tourist office out of season. There are hundreds of tourist office in the Loire but the ones listed below relate to the book's Itineraries and Options. They are normally open 10am–12pm, 2–6pm but larger ones are open all day and the Tours office stays open until late in summer.

Amboise: Quai du Général de Gaulle (Tel: 47 57 09 28).
Angers (town): Place Kennedy, Angers (Tel: 41 88 69 63).
Anjou (region): Place Kennedy, Angers (Tel: 41 88 23 85).
Azay-le-Rideau: Place de l'Europe (Tel: 47 45 44 40).
Beaugency: 28 Place du Martroi (Tel: 38 44 54 42).

Blois (town): 3 ave Jean Laigret (Tel: 54 74 06 49).
Blois (region): 11 Place du Château (Tel: 54 78 55 50).
Chambord: Château de Chambord (Tel: 54 20 31 50).
Chaumont: 45 Rue du Maréchal-Leclerc (Tel: 54 20 96 45).
Chenonceau: Château de Chenonceau (Tel: 47 23 90 07).
Chinon: 12 Rue Voltaire (Tel: 47 93 17 85).
Cour-Cheverny: 4 Avenue de la République (Tel: 54 79 95 63).
Loches: Place de la Marne (Tel: 47 59 07 98).
Montreuil-Bellay: 34 Rue du Marché (Tel: 41 52 32 39).
Orléans (and Orléanais): Place Albert I (Tel: 38 53 05 95).
Romorantin-Lanthenay (and Sologne): (Tel: 54 76 43 89).
Saumur: Place de la Bilange (Tel: 41 51 03 06).
Tours: Boulevard Heurteloup (Tel: 47 05 58 08).
Touraine (region): 9 Rue Buffon, Tours (Tel: 47 31 48 10).

FURTHER READING

For background reading the *Insight Guide: Loire Valley* (Apa Publications, 1990) offers in-depth essays on the region including a detailed history and articles on Loire literature and rural life. The liveliest individual châteaux guides are surprisingly published by the French Ministry of Culture (Editions Ouest France) and are often found in English. These are the booklets to choose when a particular château captures your imagination. Pierre Boille's *Le Vieux Tours* (Nouvelle République) describes a delightful walking tour through old Tours.

For exhaustive analysis of every church and château, get *Le Guide Bleu: Centre, Châteaux de la Loire* (Hachette). *The Loire Valley* (Michelin Guide Vert) is a handy reference book with good routes. For a comprehensive series on the Loire Valley's individual regions, try the *Encyclopédies Régionales* (Editions Christine Bonneton). The most atmospheric one is *Touraine*. If social history appeals, read Ivan Cloulas' *La Vie Quotidienne dans les Châteaux de la Loire au Temps de la Renaissance* (Hachette), an account of the Loire's most glorious period.

Guy Breton's *Amours Secrets* (Nouvelle République) provides romantic speculation about kings, queens and royal mistresses in the Loire. Isabelle Duvivier's *Guide Littéraire du Val de Loire* (Nouvelle République) is a good introduction to Balzac, Rabelais and the other great writers from the Loire. John Ardagh's *Writer's France* covers the same ground. To recreate the flavour of the Loire in your kitchen, read *Recettes du Val de Loire* (Nouvelle République). If the Loire wines have gone to your head, the wine bible is the yearly *Le Guide Hachette des Vins* (Hachette), complete with recommended visits to wine-growers. In case you are already planning another trip, get *French Country Welcome* (Fivédit, Paris), a description of recommended *chambres d'hôtes* throughout France.

Index

A

Agincourt 14, 17
Alcuin 10
Amboise 1, 11, 12, 16, 17, 34, 35, 42, 43, 79, 82, 85, 88, 90
Angers 10, 11, 12, 15, 16, 17, 60, 67, 68, 70, 71, 73, 75, 76, 77, 79, 80, 81, 82, 85, 88, 89, 90
Anjou 10, 11, 12, 15, 16, 17, 56, 60, 62, 64, 72, 73–4, 82, 88, 89
   wine 26, 62, 68, 69, 77
Aquitaine 12
Artannes 89
Asnières 12
Auvergne 12
Avoine 17
Azay-le-Rideau 1, 8, 13, 50–1, 53, 57, 79, 82, 89, 90

B

Balzac, Honoré de 1, 8, 13, 46, 53–4, 61, 76, 80, 89, 91
Beauce, La 21, 28–30
Beaucouzé 89
Beaugency 1, 17, 19, 20–1, 25, 30, 31, 79, 82, 89, 90
Berry 15, 75
Bessé 66

Blésois 15, 72
Blois 1, 11, 12, 16, 17, 18, 20, 25, 29, 31, 32–3, 36–8, 39, 44, 72, 79, 80, 81, 85, 88, 89, 91
Bohalle, La 74
Bourbons 17
Bourgueil 9, 12, 16, 55–6, 69, 81, 82
   wine 1, 55–6, 74, 77, 78
Bréhémont 13, 51, 57
Brissac 68, 77, 82
Brottières 15
Burgundians 14, 28
Bury 39

C

Candes-St-Martin 12, 17, 58–9
Capetian dynasty 10, 17
Chambord 9, 12, 13, 17, 19, 20, 22–3, 30, 31, 32, 79–80, 81, 82, 85, 88, 89, 90, 91
Charlemagne 10, 17
Charles VII 11, 34, 77
Charles VIII 12, 14, 17, 40, 77
Château de la Grille 55
Château des Réaux 16
Château du Moulin 40
Château Dunois 21
Chaumont 13, 33–4, 42, 44, 88, 90, 91
Chédigny 80

Chémery 8, 41
Chênehutte-les-Tuffeaux 66, 69
Chenonceaux 48, 82
Chenonceau, château de 1, 13, 14, 18, 19, 34, 43–5, 50, 80, 90, 91
Cher, river 1, 14, 38, 44, 45, 49, 90
Cheverny 13, 20, 23–5, 80, 85, 88, 90
  wine 25, 77
Chinon 9, 10, 11, 12, 14, 16, 17, 51, 52, 55, 57, 58, 59, 81, 82, 89, 90, 91
  wine 46, 48, 52, 55, 56, 74, 77, 78
Cisse, river 42
Clos Lucé 16, 17, 34, 35, 90
Cointreau 68, 71, 74
Compiègne 14
Contres 31
Coteaux de Layon 77
Cour-Cheverny 23, 31, 88, 91
Cour-sur-Loire 30
Crécy 17
Cunault 10, 12, 62, 66, 67, 81, 82, 89

D, E, F

Daguenière, La 74
Dénézé-sous-Doué 63
Devinière, La 58
Doué-la-Fontaine 62, 82, 90
Etang de Bézard 40, 89
Ferté-St-Aubin, La 82
Fondettes 48
Fontevraud L'Abbaye 10, 12, 60, 61, 65, 69, 80, 82
Fosse, La 63
François I 11, 12–13, 17, 22, 23, 32, 34, 35, 36, 38, 45, 51
François II 17, 2
French Revolution 13, 17, 23, 28, 36, 68

G

Gascony 12
Gennes 66
Gien 14, 70, 71
Grange de Meslay 80, 81
Guines 17
Guise, Duc de 33

H, I, J

Henri II 13, 34, 44
Henri III 33, 45, 60
Henri IV 33
Henry II (Plantagenet) 10, 12, 17, 22, 59
Henry V 17
Huismes 51, 52, 57
Hundred Years War 11, 17, 21
Hurault family 23–4
Indre, river 30, 48, 50, 51, 53, 54, 90
Joan of Arc 11, 14, 17, 21, 25, 26, 27, 28, 47, 80, 81

L

Langeais 17, 57
Lassay-sur-Croisne 40
Leonardo da Vinci 11, 16, 17, 22, 34–5, 38, 90
Loches 11–12, 13, 14, 17, 80, 82, 91
Louis VII 17, 22
Louis XI 11, 12, 34
Louis XII 12, 17, 32, 36, 38
Louis XIII 33
Louis XIV 13, 17
Louis XV 43
Louis XX 15
Louresse-Rochemenier 63
Lude, Le 79, 80

M

Maine 12, 88
Marçay 57
Marmoutier Abbey 17
Maves 29–30
Médicis, Catherine de 13, 33, 34, 44, 45, 64
Ménars 30
Monsoreau 60
Montlouis 82, 78
Montreuil-Bellay 62, 64–6, 69, 88, 89, 91
Muides-sur-Loire 31
Mulsans 30
Mur-de-Sologne 39
Muscadet 78

N, O, P

Napoleon III 39
Nevers 70
Normandy 121
Notre Dame de Cléry 14, 21
Onzain 33, 42
Orléanais 15, 72, 91
Orléans 10, 11, 14, 15, 17, 25–8, 38, 44, 70, 71, 72, 75, 76, 81, 82, 85, 89, 91
Pagode de Chanteloup 43
Parnay 8, 89
Philippe I 17
Plantagenets 10, 12, 17, 52, 59, 61, 66
Plessis-les-Tours 12
Poitou 12
Pont de Ruan 53

R, S

René, King 11, 61, 62
Rheims 14
Richard I Lionheart 12, 52, 59
Roman de la Rose 10
Romorantin-Lanthenay 41, 82, 89, 91
Rouen 14, 17, 71
Saché 53–4, 80, 82
Saint-Symphorien 84
Santiago de Compostela 22, 62
Saumur 1, 8, 12, 14, 17, 18, 19, 60–2, 69, 71, 74, 78, 81, 82, 88, 89, 91
Savonnières 49
Sologne, La 8, 15, 21, 38–41, 71, 72, 74, 75, 89, 91
son et lumière 8, 24, 35, 51, 79–80, 81, 84, 85, 90
Suèvres 30

T, U

Talcy 29, 30
Thouet, river 1, 64, 88, 90
Touraine 8, 12, 13, 15, 16, 43–8, 53, 54, 56, 57, 69, 71, 72, 73, 74, 88, 91
  wine 23, 33, 78
Tournus 67
Tours 10, 12, 14, 15, 17, 36, 45–7, 48, 53, 70, 71, 73, 75, 76, 79, 80, 81, 82, 85, 88, 89, 90, 91
Trèves 66, 67, 82
troglodytes 1, 8, 54, 60, 61, 62–4, 90
Troussay 39
Turquant 60, 64
Ussé 16, 19, 51–2, 90

V, W

Valois dynasty 13
Veigné 48
Veilleins 40
Vendôme 17, 21, 85
Versailles 17, 18, 23, 32, 33
Vienne, river 55, 58
Villaines-les-Rochers 54, 71
Villandry 9, 13, 19, 49–50, 57?
Villesavin 9, 49
Villexanton 29
Villiers 29
Vouvray 8, 48, 81, 82
  wine 1, 74, 77, 78
Wars of Religion 13, 17, 28, 33, 67
wine 8, 9, 10, 15, 16, 23, 25, 26, 39, 42, 46, 48, 55, 56, 60, 65, 66–7, 69, 76–8, 77, 81, 82, 90, 91
wine-tasting 15, 25, 55, 65, 66, 68, 77

Art & Photo Credits

Photography **Lyle Lawson**
Publisher **Hans Höfer**
Design Concept **V Barl**
Designer **Klaus Geisler**
Managing Editor **Andrew Eames**
Cartography **Berndtson & Berndtson**

TAKE THE EASY WAY OUT, TO HOLIDAY FRANCE..

USE THE BYPASS.

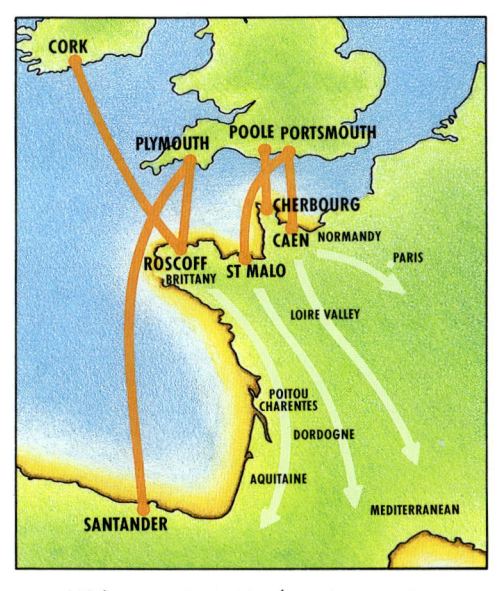

We've easy to get to departure ports, with convenient sailings and civilised ships. And the most modern fleet on the Channel. We sail direct to Brittany, Normandy & Spain and bypass busy Dover, Calais & Le Havre. And we've a huge range of great value holidays and breaks, too. We're the better value way, from the winners of the 1991 Observer 'Favourite Ferry' Award.

Brittany Ferries
Take the easy way out

FOR BROCHURES RING **(0705) 751708** NOW.
FOR RESERVATIONS RING **(0705) 827701** OR SEE YOUR TRAVEL AGENT.

INSIGHT GUIDES

COLORSET NUMBERS

160 Alaska	204 East African Wildlife	100 New England
155 Alsace	149 Eastern Europe,	184E New Orleans
150 Amazon Wildlife	118 Ecuador	184F New York City
116 America, South	148A Edinburgh	133 New York State
173 American Southwest	268 Egypt	293 New Zealand
158A Amsterdam	123 Finland	265 Nile, The
260 Argentina	209B Florence	120 Norway
287 Asia, East	243 Florida	124B Oxford
207 Asia, South	154 France	147 Pacific Northwest
262 Asia, South East	135C Frankfurt	205 Pakistan
194 Asian Wildlife, Southeast	208 Gambia & Senegal	154A Paris
167A Athens	135 Germany	249 Peru
272 Australia	148B Glasgow	184B Philadelphia
263 Austria	279 Gran Canaria	222 Philippines
188 Bahamas	169 Great Barrier Reef	115 Poland
206 Bali Baru	124 Great Britain	202 Portugal
107 Baltic States	167 Greece	114A Prague
246A Bangkok	166 Greek Islands	153 Provence
292 Barbados	135G Hamburg	156 Puerto Rico
219B Barcelona	240 Hawaii	250 Rajasthan
187 Bay of Naples	193 Himalaya, Western	177 Rhine
234A Beijing	196 Hong Kong	127C Rio de Janeiro
109 Belgium	144 Hungary	172 Rockies
135A Berlin	256 Iceland	209A Rome
217 Bermuda	247 India	101 Russia
100A Boston	212 India, South	275B San Francisco
127 Brazil	128 Indian Wildlife	130 Sardinia
178 Brittany	143 Indonesia	148 Scotland
109A Brussels	142 Ireland	184D Seattle
144A Budapest	252 Israel	261 Sicily
260A Buenos Aires	236A Istanbul	159 Singapore
213 Burgundy	209 Italy	257 South Africa
268A Cairo	213 Jamaica	264 South Tyrol
247B Calcutta	278 Japan	219 Spain
275 California	266 Java	220 Spain, Southern
180 California, Northern	252A Jerusalem-Tel Aviv	105 Sri Lanka
161 California, Southern	203A Kathmandu	101B St Petersburg
237 Canada	270 Kenya	170 Sweden
162 Caribbean The Lesser Antilles	300 Korea	232 Switzerland
122 Catalonia (Costa Brava)	202A Lisbon	272 Sydney
141 Channel Islands	258 Loire Valley	175 Taiwan
184C Chicago	124A London	112 Tenerife
151 Chile	275A Los Angeles	186 Texas
234 China	201 Madeira	246 Thailand
135E Cologne	219A Madrid	278A Tokyo
119 Continental Europe	145 Malaysia	139 Trinidad & Tobago
189 Corsica	157 Mallorca & Ibiza	113 Tunisia
281 Costa Rica	117 Malta	236 Turkey
291 Cote d'Azur	272B Melbourne	171 Turkish Coast
165 Crete	285 Mexico	210 Tuscany
184 Crossing America	285A Mexico City	174 Umbria
226 Cyprus	243A Miami	237A Vancouver
114 Czechoslovakia	237B Montreal	198 Venezuela
247A Delhi, Jaipur, Agra	235 Morocco	209C Venice
238 Denmark	101A Moscow	263A Vienna
135B Dresden	135D Munich	255 Vietnam
142B Dublin	211 Myanmar (Burma)	267 Wales
135F Düsseldorf	259 Namibia	184C Washington DC
	269 Native America	183 Waterways of Europe
	203 Nepal	215 Yemen
	158 Netherlands	

You'll find the colorset number on the spine of each Insight Guide.

INSIGHT POCKET GUIDES

EXISTING & FORTHCOMING TITLES:

Aegean Islands	Ireland	Phuket
Algarve	Istanbul	Prague
Alsace	**J**akarta	Provence
Athens	**K**athmandu	**R**hodes
Bali	*Bikes & Hikes*	Rome
Bali Bird Walks	Kenya	**S**abah
Bangkok	Kuala Lumpur	San Francisco
Barcelona	**L**isbon	Sardinia
Bavaria	Loire Valley	Scotland
Berlin	London	Seville/Grenada
Bhutan	**M**acau	Seychelles
Boston	Madrid	Sikkim
Brittany	Malacca	Singapore
Brussels	Mallorca	South California
Budapest &	Malta	Southeast England
Surroundings	Marbella/	Sri Lanka
Canton	*Costa del Sol*	St Petersburg
Chiang Mai	Miami	Sydney
Costa Blanca	Milan	**T**enerife
Costa Brava	Morocco	Thailand
Cote d'Azur	Moscow	Tibet
Crete	Munich	Turkish Coast
Denmark	**N**epal	Tuscany
Florence	New Delhi	**V**enice
Florida	New York City	Vienna
Gran Canaria	North California	**Y**ogyakarta
Hawaii	**O**slo/Bergen	Yugoslavia's
Hong Kong	**P**aris	*Adriatic Coast*
Ibiza	Penang	

- - - - - - - - - - - - - - - -

United States: Houghton Mifflin Company, Boston MA 02108
Tel: (800) 2253362 Fax: (800) 4589501

Canada: Thomas Allen & Son, 390 Steelcase Road East
Markham, Ontario L3R 1G2
Tel: (416) 4759126 Fax: (416) 4756747

Great Britain: GeoCenter UK, Hampshire RG22 4BJ
Tel: (256) 817987 Fax: (256) 817988

Worldwide: Höfer Communications Singapore 2262
Tel: (65) 8612755 Fax: (65) 8616438

" I was first drawn to the Insight Guides by the excellent "Nepal" volume. I can think of no book which so effectively captures the essence of a country. Out of these pages leaped the Nepal I know – the captivating charm of a people and their culture. I've since discovered and enjoyed the entire Insight Guide Series. Each volume deals with a country or city in the same sensitive depth, which is nowhere more evident than in the superb photography. "

Sir Edmund Hillary

NOTES